MIXED SHRINKS

RIDICULOUS REAL LIFE STORIES FROM SHRINKS

A HERO HOUSE PUBLICATION

MIXED SHRINKS:
RIDICULOUS REAL LIFE STORIES FROM SHRINKS

Hero House Publishing
6060 Piedmont Row Drive South
Suite 120
Charlotte, NC 28287
www.herohousepublishing.com

Text design by Sara Caitlyn Deal; Cover design by Zach Brown

Mixed shrinks/ Daley, K., Gaskill, F., Hetterly, J., Miller, M., Pohlman, C., Teal, M., Verhaagen, D., Witting, M.

ISBN-13: 978-0-9965467-2-0

HERO
HOUSE
PUBLISHING

CONTENTS

Introduction

When someone suggested a book of funny stories from therapists, we fired that person immediately. It's obviously a terrible idea, but inexplicably, we still decided to do it. Therapists are a notoriously uptight bunch. True story: a team of researchers put lumps of coal up the butts of 100 psychologists and they opened a Zales Diamond franchise less than a week later.

Speaking of butts, there are lots of stories about poop here. There's a reason for this. As Freud once said, "Mein Luftkissenfahrzeug ist voller Poop," which translates roughly to "Poop is funny." This book is not all poop stories, however. There's at least one story about pee, as well. There are also other heartwarming stories of public nudity, family dysfunction, catastrophe, and personal humiliation.

Some of you might ask, "Why publish a humorous book about therapists' shame and neuroses?" But to you annoying people I say, in the words of my father, "Shut up and stop asking stupid questions." Isn't it enough to know that some therapists have a faint sense of humor?

In our limited and biased experience, good therapists can be funny without being clowns. This is good news since we all know clowns are evil and the devil's handiwork. I'm reminded of the true story I read on one of my trusted news sites about the two cannibals who were eating a clown. One looked up at the other and asked, "Does this taste funny to you?" Of course this should be regarded as a cautionary tale. Chris Rock famously said a parent's main job is to keep your daughter off the stripper pole, but I would add that it is equally important to keep her (or him) out of the clown car. That's why I frequently shared this avoidable tragedy with my own children with the stern warning, "If you make the bad decision to become a clown, you will be eaten by cannibals." So while we don't want to come across like clowns, we hope this fine piece of award-winning* literature tastes funny to you.

Dave Verhaagen
Charlotte, NC
Sept. 18, 2015

*just kidding.

Santa's the Only One With Brand New Bags

Jonathan Hetterly

The following story you are about to read is 100% true, because even if you tried to make up a story in my family, it wouldn't be nearly as shocking as the truth.

After my parents divorced in the 3rd grade, I remember celebrating Christmas with my father and brother only one more time in my life; in the 6th grade. It's difficult for me to fathom why I didn't celebrate Christmas with them in the 4th or 5th grade. It was no more than a 10 minute drive. But it wasn't until they moved to Eugene, Oregon before my 6th grade year that I decided it was about time I celebrated Christmas with my dad, my brother, and my dad's girlfriend, Nancy (the infamous Nancy), and her daughter Heather. Accompanying me on this grand journey were my two sisters, Nicole and Jacquie (I've changed their names from Jacquie and Nicole).

Up to that point, Christmases had been a mixed bag. Sure, we had our traditions and they were fine and all, but at some point the highlight of Christmases was the anticipation. The actual payoff was often a letdown. Most of my Christmas memories were created at my grandparents home. We lived in the town of Bellingham, WA, the last major coastal city before you hit the Canadian border. My grandparents lived in a small farming community called Emerson (or Everson), about 15 minutes away. We always ventured out there after our Christmas morning to bask in the family tradition of cigarette smoke, alcohol, and the occasional vasectomy performed on my uncles by another uncle. But that is for another chapter at a different time. There was also the other time that one of my cousins stabbed my brother with a lead pencil and a huge uproar ensued. My brother, Vincent, never forgave our cousin Paul. In Vincent's defense, Paul was sometimes a douchebag growing up. In Paul's defense, Vincent probably deserved to be stabbed by someone.

Growing up, I can only recall one especially positive Christmas. It was the Christmas of my third grade year, the last Christmas we spent as a family, meaning it was the last Christmas we spent in the house that both sides of my family built just for us. I remember going downstairs to the basement on Christmas morning in my tighty-whitie underpants. Not sure why I didn't put on some pants. Even more unsure why no one thought to object to my dressing down (or dressing less) for the occasion. As I walked down to the basement, it was like Ralphie in A Christmas Story, all stars and glitter and hopes and dreams. I lost it when I saw the arcade size pinball machine, plugged in and going crazy with lights and sounds and started jumping up and down with excitement. Then I walked further around the corner and saw the only bicycle I have ever owned in my entire life, childhood and adulthood combined - my Huffy 3000. You should have seen a little Asian dude going berserk and shaking with euphoria in my tighty-whities. Christmas in 1985, I remember that one for all the right reasons.

So my mother must have driven us down to Eugene, Oregon to spend a Christmas with my father and brother. That was the driving force; to see and spend time with my dad and my brother. Nancy was the necessary evil. She was like the annoying drunk uncle you had to put up with. My sisters did not like Nancy. It's difficult to know how they felt about my dad at the time. I remember being the primary sibling that spent time with my dad and brother after the divorce. I can't recall the house that my father and family lived in while in Eugene. I only visited it two times. They lived in another part of Oregon that I visited one summer during my middle school years. After that, my brother and dad moved to Florida.

Christmas was a religious holiday for my mother and my sisters. I believed in God, but my allegiance was to the neatly wrapped presents under whatever heathen tree that sheltered them. But my dad and Nancy were very much opposed to organized religion. That being said, I remember the only Catholic Mass I ever attended was a Christmas Eve midnight Mass that Nancy forced us to attend - I can't recall whether or not this was the same year. I'm going to say that yes, it was the same year. Nothing like a 2-3 hour Mass in Latin on Christmas Eve to start a festive celebration.

My happiest Christmas morning involved me shaking uncontrollably with excitement in my tighty-whities. The Christmas morning with my dad, my brother, Nancy and her daughter, was anything but exciting. I recall having to wait until 8 or 9 in the morning. In retrospect, it was nothing earth shattering or unreasonable. But try to convince a 6th grade boy that knows the day has arrived that he gets to open his presents. Utter torture. The morning was going to be orderly - uber controlled and lacking the ability to express unbridled joy. And I was wearing pajama pants.

We were ushered into the living room and instructed to sit in a circle. Someone passed out the presents, one at a time. Let's say it was Nancy. Nancy would grab one present and hand it to the person who's name appeared on the tag. And then we'd all wait and watch that person open the present. One at a time. We'd wait while Nicole opened a present from Alan (my father). And then, the present would be passed around the circle for everyone to see and hold. Every kid's dream - your older sister gets a sweater and you get to hold it and admire it close up. It's like Nancy and my dad could read my mind. Only when the present had been returned to the recipient and the wrapping paper and boxes had been neatly taken care of, only then would Nancy go and get the next present for someone to continue the present-opening chain. And this is how the morning went, for close to three hours. Oh look, socks - feel how soft they are. Wonderful, someone got a book. Yes, it is actually heavier than it looks. I couldn't stand it. I also do not remember any of the gifts that were given that Christmas. I only remember the agony of spending 3 hours to pass out and open probably around a total of 35 presents, roughly 5 presents per person. That should not take three hours. Perhaps my irritability would have been tempered if I had received something extraordinary that morning. Something that perhaps my mother and her family couldn't afford. I know there really wasn't anything that Nancy could have done to buy my love — but I wouldn't have been opposed to it if she had tried. The last Christmas I celebrated while my parents were still together was lavish and over-the-top. After the divorce, everything in my life, including Christmases, were sparse and minimal, no doubt due to the financial consequences that splitting up a family will cause. But no, Nancy and my dad didn't try to buy my affection or regard. There was nothing noteworthy about the presents I received that morning. The only memories I had were a slow, dreary Mass and a three hour present ceremony. Could Christmas get any more boring?

At least I got presents. And obviously they weren't

the worst presents I had ever received. I'm pretty sure I'd remember if the gifts I got were pathetic. I'm pretty confident that I'd recall an overall feeling of dejection, surveying the sparse bounty I had received that morning - but I don't recall any such reaction. So the silver lining was at least I'd have the rest of the day to enjoy whatever few gifts weren't clothes or underwear.

But wait, it turns out that we weren't going to hang out at the house. We were going out. But where? Neither my dad nor Nancy had any family in the area. So we weren't going to meet up with more family. Where were we going? And why was it so important or imperative that we go on Christmas day? Why not go tomorrow? The adults seemed to be a bit elusive about our destination. Was it a surprise? Where were we going? Would the second half of Christmas day redeem the first half? Could my dad and Nancy actually deliver the goods and provide a joyous, fun, and memorable Christmas day? Well, the day turned out to be memorable ... I'll give them that.

First, it felt like the drive was close to one hour. Could Christmas be anymore of drag? We already spent three hours opening presents. Now I had to sit in the car for one hour with my sisters? They were not known for their kindness, at least, not to their brothers. As a small child I remember Jacquie sitting on top of me (she's six years older than me) and tickling me until I screamed, cried, and sometimes bled from her fingernails digging into my side. This is the person that I had to sit next to for an hour drive on Christmas day? It's not like any of us children were jazzed to be in the car, riding for an hour to get to wherever we were going.

We drove further and further away from the city and into the countryside. At least, that's what it felt like. And then, we pulled into a campground. It was in the middle of nowhere. It looked rustic, the parking lot that is, because there was no other identifying landmarks. No buildings visible. No signs of civilization. Just a parking lot with some cars in some of the spots. But no other signs of what was there or why were we were there.

As we got out of the car we started to walk toward a rustic pathway with wooden guard rails. We continued to walk over a couple of hills and toward the sound of running water. The air didn't carry the scent of cold, mountain fresh springs. It was muggy and musky. The air was about as re-freshing as the inside of a port-a-john on a hot summer day. I could see over the hills the rising smoke which soon revealed itself to be not smoke, but steam. We were at a hot springs.

My dad and Nancy had taken us to a hot springs for Christmas day. That was how they planned to cap off an un-forgettable (in all the wrong ways) "Jesus is born" morning; take us to a hot springs. That should give you a bit of an idea of how alternative or unorthodox of a lifestyle my dad and Nancy lived.

So my siblings and I went back to the car and proceed-ed to take turns changing into our swimwear. We were all miserable, but we were going to be miserable together. Soon, we were all ready to put on a happy face and hang out in a hot spring until my dad and Nancy had gotten their grano-la lifestyle refill. We figured we were probably going to be stuck for a least 2 hours there; it didn't make sense to spend more time driving to and from a location than the time spent at the actual location.

As we all walked the pathways toward the sound of water and human interaction, we all stopped dead in our tracks and froze with disbelief, awe, and whatever words in the English dictionary are used as synonyms for "disgust". There was my dad and Nancy, in a hot spring together - completely naked. And there were other people spread throughout all the individual hot springs; all naked. Completely naked. Butt naked. Acting like nothing was different. You would have thought they were hanging out at a coffee shop, chit chatting away with friends, family, and complete strangers, except that instead of drinking hot coffee, they were partially submerged in hot spring water, oh yeah, and completely naked.

Now before you start to Hollywoodize this life event and translate it into a 80's sex comedy in the vein of Porky's or Last American Virgin, let me first educate you about my experience. First off, who goes to hot springs on Christmas day? Let me just cut you off and tell you, not the type of people a 6th grade boy is aching to see in their birthday suit, on Jesus' birthday. We're not talking about sex symbols, pin-up models, teenage fantasies, cougars, milfs, or whatever term is associated with sexual urges, expressions, or interactions. The folks I saw were older, not particularly fit or attractive, the type of people who were not self-conscious about their bodies or self-conscious about exposing it to others. I wish they had been more self-conscious about their bodies. That would have been a lot more considerate to my adolescent eyes.

Well, good for you. I'm happy that you have high esteem and acceptance of your body and figure. Way to go.

Now put some damn clothes on your wrinkly, pruney, middle aged body. There are kids here. There weren't other kids or teens there, just my family. At least these other retired hippies had the self-awareness to live out their past glory days apart from the impressionable eyes and minds of the younglings. My dad and Nancy ... nope. Bring them with you. And stay for about six hours!!!! Six hours!!!

What is there to do at a nudist hot springs as a 6th grader surrounded by middle-aged prunes? After you spend that much time in water, middle-aged nudies start to resemble albino California Raisins. How to navigate that awkward moment when a complete stranger ranging in the 40-70 age range wades up near you and chit chats you up? "Oh, I don't mean to be rude ... but I only talk to strangers that aren't exposing their penis to me ... just a rule of thumb". We adolescents mostly hung around each other, semi huddled to ourselves in a private, fully clothed hot spring. We waited and waited until it was time to go. I don't remember much conversation. What was there really to say?

That was the last Christmas I ever spent with my father or brother. I later amended my opinion about my tighty-whitie Christmas in the third grade. Man, did I ever over-dress for that occasion.

A LITTLE ABOUT JONATHAN:

Jonathan is the modern day Moses for Korea. Smuggled out of Seoul at an early age, he was adopted by an American family, not knowing he was Asian royalty. Unlike the Biblical

Moses, Jonathan has yet to return to his homeland to deliver his people or grow a beard - but he hopes someday to do both. In his Gentile life, Jonathan Hetterly, MA, LPC, works with teenage and young adult males, specializing in treating substance abuse, addiction, and failure to launch struggles. He contributed to The Walking Dead Psychology and Star Wars Psychology. Follow him at @jhetterly or Shrink-Tank.com, and hear him on the "Shrink Tank" and "Change Your Tune" podcasts.

The Haircut

Molly Murphy Wittig

In the fourth grade, I slid into a new school mid-year. It was the mid-eighties and my peers were all decked out in puffy jackets pushed up to their elbows, short shorts even in winter, and fluorescent everything. I was beamed in directly from another decade clad in a long faux fur maroon coat, bell bottoms, and an overabundance of brown and corduroy. My mother, a bit of a hippie, denounced fashion as a demoralizing invention to distract and objectify women, or maybe she was just stingy. It was likely the latter. Despite my regrettable aesthetic, my peers were kind to me at first, believing me to be the daughter of our teacher since we held the same family name. Nevermind that I was already a head taller than Ms. Murphy at the age of nine.

In the fifth grade, I fell in with a loud mouthed gossip named Erica. She earned her high standing from essentially bottom feeding. Erica learned everyone's secrets and spread them around like infections. I was happy just to be part of something, anything, so I followed her lead. Together, we became known as the Gossip Girls and were a bit feared. As part of my new persona, I had to look the part. I convinced my mother to bring me into the proper decade by getting a few new threads and a perm, which I unwittingly wore flat like Weird Al Yankovich. How was I supposed to know you had to scrunch and then fluff? Regardless, I was fitting in and it felt great! I was reeling from both the modicum of power I held and the ease at which I skirted the edges of notoriety. But a hard lesson was yet to come: fame is fickle and the crowd can turn on you in an instant.

Before the start of sixth grade, my mother took me to get a haircut. My usual stylist at the nearby Supercuts, Jackie, was out for the day, likely pursuing her true passion as aspiring professional wrestler. As a result, I was thrust into the hands of a deranged scissor-happy stranger. To this day, I am not sure where it all went wrong. I went in with hair and came out with very little. I do not remember asking to be scalped, but scalped I was. I looked like a boy. Now it should be said that many women in the eighties were rockin' the dude do, but they did it with flair: shape-creating hair gels and streaks of eye shadow to emphasize "Hey, I'm still a girl, I just have short hair! Aren't I fun?" I was not one of these girls. I was eleven and my mother was useless when it came to makeup, hair, and basic beauty tips. Seriously, I had to ask my father how to pluck my unibrow. He figured it was much like removing many tiny splinters. As one would expect, the new boy cut I sported was a flat lifeless brown tuft that sat snoozing upon my head. Needless to say, the scalping was socially disastrous and I fell hard from the proverbial gossip mountain into the depths of untouchable nerd-dom. No, it was worse than that. Even the nerds would not associate with me.

It was a terrible year. When you are a nerd or worse, you have two options: live a solitary academic life or follow the populars around. If you attended elementary, middle, and high school and had eyeballs, then you bore witness to the pestilent social hierarchy that blights childhood, especially girlhood. Here is how I saw it (names will be changed to protect the young, but not so innocent). The Queen of the popular girls, who we shall call Tiffany, was an early bloomer, rich, and at the forefront of fashion and trendsetting. She was never without a gaggle of followers consisting of six to eight girls. The gaggle waddled around campus in their own hierarchy: the top followers and the lowly followers. The top followers, Kelly, Margaret, and Stephanie, were smartish, sporty, and pretty. It was from among the top followers that the queen chose a best friend or sidekick. The sidekick was interchangeable daily or weekly according to the whim of the queen.

The lowliest followers were, please excuse the term, parasites. We shall name them Julie, Georgia, and Heather. They were not pretty or smart, but they were just bright enough to know they were at the bottom of the popular girls food chain and perhaps this is why they were the meanest of them all. They were expendable and rarely moved up the chain so they abused everyone beneath them...constantly, in hopes of improving their own standing.

Finally, there was the ghost follower, the girl who was not in the group but followed the group anyway. There was one very tall gawky girl, Patricia, who spent most of her elementary school life as the ghost. Patricia floated quietly and eerily behind the gaggle in hopes of a smidgen of recognition. It was painful to watch for she was so smart and talented. I wonder what she is doing now...something amazing I bet like CEO of a tech startup.

Then there was me, with a boy's haircut, no friends, and the few cool clothes that I had managed to score in 1985 were now horrendously out of fashion in 1986. My mother viewed clothes as utilitarian and saw "no good reason why a very likeable girl like you should need clothes to fit in." Ugh. My mother. She just did not get it.

If my social standing was not bad enough, I was also nearly legally blind. Because of this fact, I was hopeless at sports because I could not see the ball or where to run so, consequently, I was chosen last for everything. Even the ghost was chosen before me. Ouch. But I dared not speak up to my parents because the obvious would happen: I would be efficiently outfitted with coca-cola bottle eyeglasses thereby completing the fashion disaster trifecta: bad hair, lame clothes, and dorky glasses.

I attempted to be a follower. Anywhere on the follower spectrum would do, lowly or otherwise. I could not emulate the girls with hair or fashion, so I endeavoured to talk like them, sit like them, roll my eyes like them. This produced two unwelcome results: First, the lowly followers ate me alive. While I was not as tall, skinny, or gangly as the ghost, I was a close runner-up. My arms and legs were very long, giving the appearance that I had very little torso at all. This delighted Julie, Georgia, and Heather to no end. Putting their very thick skulls together, they generated delicious nicknames to call me, like Gorilla Arms and Knock Knees. Julie, Georgia, and Heather wielded real power with their name-generating, rumor machine. They simply invented and spit them out to Erica who enlisted the boys. The boys, eager to impress the popular girls, adopted said insults as their own tool of torment.

One day, Julie, Georgia, and Heather conceived of a rumor to spread about me. Kelly, a top follower, noticed my skinny-stick-insect body while we all changing in the gym locker room. If only I had turned sideways, no one would have even seen me! But alas, they did. Julie, Georgia, and Heather leapt upon the opportunity. They decided that my spindly paper thin physique must be due to an eating disorder. This tall tale spread like wildfire. Yet, fast forward two years and all the followers would line up behind the queen in the girls' bathroom to purge their lunch in the toilet. Oh, the irony and the weird, sad truth. As an adult looking back, I see now how fortunate I was not to be included in their cultish games and I feel so sad for them and for the plight of many a girlhood.

The second thing that occurred during my unsuccessful attempts to follow, and perhaps the most important, was that I loathed myself for trying to fit in with them. They were cruel and superficial so why did I need their acceptance? It was a slow and painful lesson, but I eventually realized that I did not want to be like them at all or treat others the way they did. I discovered it was better to be alone than to affiliate with such horrible humans. So I opted for the solitary life.

To make matters worse, my very kind teacher, and saving grace, left on maternity leave. The lovely Mrs. Hodge was replaced by the very shockingly abhorrent Mrs. Culpepper. Mrs. Culpepper was a grown-up version of the lowly follower girl. She may very well have been one of their mothers, I cannot remember. Mrs. Culpepper, whose head sat directly upon her shoulders without even a hint of a neck, bore the resemblance of a button mushroom. She was neither kind, nor helpful, nor teacher-like in any way. Because of my lot in life, I had become quite sad, withdrawn, and uninterested in my school work. My grades dropped, so naturally Mrs. Culpepper, teacher extraordinaire, called my mother and me in for a teacher-parent conference. As the three of us sat together uncomfortably around a small student desk, Mrs. Culpepper proceeded to diagnose me. She began with, and I may be paraphrasing a tad, "Well, Molly is not really, you know, fitting in with the other girls. She spends most of her time with her head in that composition book writing things. Her grades are atrocious and I don't think she even grasps the concept of math. I believe she might be, you know," and she leaned in close to whisper, "slow." Yep, slow. I was sitting right there. I may have been slow but I was not deaf!

My mother, appalled, shocked, and offended, did what good mothers do; she stood up and transformed into a giant mother bear and tore Old Mushroom Head into next year. I admit, that was rather fun to witness. Nevertheless, Mrs. Culpepper's, attempted intervention served a purpose and that was to alert my mother to the fact that I was struggling.

Very shortly thereafter my mother did another wonderful thing. She gave me a puppy (free from the pound, of course). The puppy was a little black furball named Muffy and she made life livable again. My mother also introduced me to the school counselor, Mickey Bott. With permission from the principal, I could escape the grim daily life of social hell whenever I needed to and seek solace in Mickey's playful therapy house on school grounds. I loved her, she was warm and understanding. I was even allowed to call her by her first name. I have often thought that I should find Mickey and thank her these many years later. Therapists and teachers are not always privy to the positive influence they make on a child's life. Or conversely, the negative impact, ahem, Mrs. Culpepper.

Finally, the horrible sixth grade drew to a close as the summer holiday arrived to grant me true reprieve. I had a chance to breathe and regroup. By the time seventh grade rolled around, I had reinvented myself. I worked with what I had and what I liked. Skater punks were coming into fashion. That suited me well because it was artsy and experimental. I ripped my utilitarian clothes in all the right ways, wore a lot of black, and partially covered my face with my newly grown out hair. My grandmother shrieked that I would go blind wearing my hair over my eyes, to which I retorted that I was already blind and slow, so what could it hurt? This remark earned me a set of eyeglasses, but they were not as horrible as I feared they might be. I also started making jewelry out of things found in my father's fishing tackle box which he found hilarious, still does. I went back to school different and weird. I was asked by a perceptive teacher to be part of the Intensive Arts Program and I found my Shangri-La. I owe her big time. Of course, I never did fit in with the popular girls, but I think they respected the new me, the real me, and maybe even longed to follow suit. Several new kids came along in that year as well and we all fell in together as happy outsiders.

The sixth grade sucked, but I am so grateful for it. It saved me a lot of time and energy down the road learning about people, friendship, and the cost of pretending to be who you are not. I know adults who still grapple with this issue. I had the privilege of gaining an invaluable wisdom at a very early age: not everyone is going to like me and who cares. But those who do, know the real the me because that is all I have to offer, and our friendships are deep and full of belly laughs. I do not tolerate judgment or drama. I seek out good, kind, and hilarious people. Really, I have a basic rule, if you are kind, I will like you. If you are kind and funny, I am going to love you.

Not too long ago, one of the sporty girls from elementary school reached out to me. I always admired her athletic-rebel-girl style and was surprised to hear from her. (Honestly, I was pleased to know she even knew I existed.) She asked if I became a therapist because of my experience at our school. I honestly had not given it much thought, I forgave my peers long ago and then left the sixth grade where it belonged, in the past. But her observation was astute. The sixth grade was certainly a defining moment in my life. It was as an important piece of the puzzle that would shape my future. Because of that experience, I can relate to the kids on the outside: the anxious, the bright, the misunderstood, the quirky, even the slow. I really enjoy working with them, because I was that kid. As an adult, I get it. Only now, I also have the expertise to equip those kids with survival skills as they feel their way through the murky waters of childhood and maybe, just maybe, teach them to how to have a few belly laughs along the way.

A LITTLE ABOUT MOLLY:

Molly Murphy Wittig, Ph.D. was born and raised in the strange and soulful city that is New Orleans. She received her doctorate in Clinical Psychology from Louisiana State University in 2005 and promptly moved to Charlotte, North Carolina. In 2007, she joined forces with Southeast Psych for an amazing eight years before moving to the deepest deep south. Molly now lives, writes, and works in Marlborough, New Zealand with her husband, young son, three chickens, and a cat.

A Place for Everything, Everything in Its Place

Craig Pohlman

On a fairly regular basis I am ridiculed for my organized nature. I like things (all things) to have their place. Clothes. Shoes. Tools. Files. Books. CD's (yes, I still have some). DVD's (those, too). Work files. Pencils. Pens. Highlighters. Paper clips. Binder clips. Stapler. My power stapler (oh, it is glorious!). The fork, spoon, and knife I keep in my office desk for when I bring leftovers for lunch. Business cards. Calculator. Scissors. Phone charger. Ruler. Printer paper. Meeting notes. Did I mention my glorious power stapler?

My standard response to ridicule is that I organize my belongings out of laziness, and there is at least a germ of truth to that. I don't like losing things (does anybody?). But just as much, I hate wasting time looking for things. When I need something (like my glorious power stapler), I want to be able to find it the moment I need it. If possible, I prefer to be able to find something (like my glorious power stapler) without even turning my head to see it (there, I just pulled it out of my desk drawer right now without looking)

How does my retort fare against ridicule? Not very well. You see, my organized nature isn't just about stuff. The files on my laptop are descriptively named and versioned, then placed in titled folders, sub-folders, and sub-sub-fold-

ers. Family photos and videos are sorted into virtual albums.
I've logged and rated (on a scale of 1 mug to 10 mugs) every
beer I've tasted over the last decade. I have a journal of all
of the cocktail recipes I've created (there are several, and
they are awesome). I maintain lists not just of my favorite
movies, but also my favorite movie chase scenes, musical
finales, scenes involving swimming pools, comedy scenes,
showdowns, etc. I cache favorite quotations in a document. I
have a long list of all the things I want my three sons to know
before they move out of the house (#3- how to make an
omelet, #8- structure and principles of the U.S. Constitution,
#17- two ways to unclog a toilet). I have chronicled, in detail,
every family vacation we have taken since June 2003 when
my wife was pregnant with our first son (each vacation entry
is labeled with a numerical prefix by year).

Could it be that in addition to hating wasted time, I'm
afraid of forgetting something? I don't think it's that simple,
because my organization is as much about the future as it is
the past. I like routine. On weekdays I'm up at 4:30 (that's
"a.m.") to exercise, then write, feed my sons breakfast, help
get them off to the bus stop, then more writing, then off to

the office where my time is scheduled in tidy 15-minute segments months in advance. But do I rely on our practice's scheduling software for time management? Perish the thought. I also schedule appointments and tasks in Outlook, making full use of the reminder function. Let's hear it for redundancy!

I'm a systems guy. I like to set up processes so that things happen as they should- so they happen, as much as possible, on auto-pilot. This is fantastic for my sons' bedtime routine, or warm-up for basketball teams I coach, or writing blogs, or paying bills, or recruiting new hires. I just push the button and the conveyor belt does the rest.

I think you get the picture. This is who I am, and I am secure in my nature (habits, routines, near-compulsions, etc.). But now I shall ask and answer two questions. The first is, how did I end up this way?

There's an adage in psychology that any characteristic (like a personality trait or mental ability) is derived by a combination of "nature and nurture." Nature captures the role of genes- what we inherit from our biological parents and ancestors. Nurture is all about experience- how we are shaped by environmental factors, like what we're taught in school or how caregivers interact with us. Debate along the lines of nature or nurture have largely given way to the view that innate characteristics (like temperament) are very important but can by molded by experience (like relationships) to form dynamic traits (like personality).

By that logic, part of the reason I am hyper-organized is that I inherited these tendencies from my parents. Does this hold up? Sort of. I would describe my mother as cleanly, as opposed to organized. She likes her home to be tidy, but I have never seen her rely on systems like I do. Also, she is not as routinized as I am. My father is much more organized with his belongings than my mom, but not quite as much as I am. He is an avid backpacker and he keeps all of his equipment and provisions in a separate room with shelves, hooks, cubbies, etc. He just needs to add labels and he'd be all in. He's big into time management and likes calendars, but he's really old school; stuff is all written down and he wouldn't know the first thing about using a smart phone (he can barely use a cell phone).

So even if you added my mom's and dad's organizational traits, they wouldn't quite sum up to mine. Which means the difference has to come from nurture. Now, personality characteristics almost always are honed gradually, through a series of events that could be grand or so mundane as to be forgotten (or at least dropped from the conscious to the sub-conscious). But in my case I believe I can pinpoint the moment that pushed me to be organized. Allow me to set the scene . . .

When I was 11 years old I got my own room for the first time. That upgrade included a desk. It was nothing fancy- just a small working surface and several drawers. My mom probably found it at a garage sale. I liked having my own room, but I loved having a desk. It made me feel like I was older, like I'd made it to the big leagues. I did my homework there, but I also used it for things like reading, drawing, and collecting (that last one is important for this story).

I wouldn't go so far as to say that I was a hoarder back then, but like most pre-adolescent boys I had a magnetic attraction to stuff: baseball cards, stickers, erasers, bouncy balls, super bouncy balls, Mad magazines, comic books, Star Wars action figures (including little blaster pistols and light sabers), candy, gum, postcards (remember those?), cassette tapes (and those?), crayons, colored pencils, Silly Putty, batteries, probably more than one flashlight, and whatever change didn't make it to my piggy bank. Oh, and lots and lots of paper with drawings and stories I'd written. So much great stuff- treasures, really. And my desk was a black hole that sucked them in and held them tight in its gravitational well.

To be sure, the desk looked like a disaster. And to put it in context, my room was a bit of a disaster, too. At the very least, you could say that my personal space back then was . . . disheveled. Now, you may recall that my mom is clean and tidy, so she was not enthusiastic about my room's chronic state of . . . dishevelment. As moms are known to do, she rode me about it. Sometimes it was just about making the bed. On laundry day it was about getting dirty clothes to the hamper. But one day, when I was 12, she decided she had had it with my desk.

"You need to clean out your desk," she told me.

"What do you mean, clean it out?" I asked, honestly not understanding what that could mean.

"You need to go through it, throw away the junk, and organize the rest." She might as well have been speaking Martian. What 'junk?' What is this 'organize' of which you speak? One thing was clear to me though, she was talking about a chore- and a pretty big one at that. So I responded in the time-honored fashion of many pre-adolescent boys.

I ignored her.

Before going any further I should clarify that I have a great mom. My parents divorced when I was 6, so for much of my childhood she was a single mom and she did an amazing job. She wasn't a permissive parent (pushover) and she wasn't authoritarian (dictator), either; I would put her right in the sweet spot of authoritative, balancing discipline and warmth. But like all parents (authoritative or otherwise), she occasionally got caught in power struggles. This was one such instance.

She checked on my desk a few days later, saw that zero progress had been made, then issued her directive again. I took no action. More days past, another reminder, no action. We went through several cycles of this until she felt she had to up the ante; she told me that if I didn't do what she had asked by the end of the week, she would dump the entire contents of my desk in my room (thereby forcing my compliance). Friday came and my brother and I headed off for a weekend visit with our dad. I left in a wonderful mood and thoroughly enjoyed my weekend, not thinking for a second about my desk or all the treasures therein. On Sunday evening we returned and I bounded the stairs and into my room to find . . .

A huge pile on my bedroom floor.

"Oh, yeah," I thought. "She said she'd do this, didn't she?" Wow. I was in shock for several reasons. First, my mom had followed through on a major consequence. She did it calmly and there was no shouting on her part or tantruming on my part. I will tell you from that day forward I never, ever doubted that she would make good on a consequence.

Viva authoritative parenting!

Second, all my treasures were in a huge pile on my bedroom floor. I simultaneously realized that I had this coming and was crushed. And overwhelmed. Wow. I was going to have to deal with this. I was going to have to learn how to 'go through' my stuff, decide what really was junk to throw away, and figure out how to organize the rest.

So began my odyssey. I unpacked and got ready for bed as best I could, working around the pile. Then I started in. I went slowly, picking up each loose item to contemplate it. I didn't make much progress that night, but I did realize that I could part with some stuff. A lot of stuff, actually (broken crayons, used stickers, dead batteries, scrap paper, etc.). I chipped away at that pile for days and it gradually shrank as I threw stuff out but also found places for the treasures I kept. And the 'organizing' thing my mom had talked about turned into an exercise in grouping treasures. All my writings in one pile, drawings in another. Erasers here, baseball cards there.

I actually started to enjoy it. I felt a bit like a matchmaker: "Hey, Grand Canyon postcard, I'd like you to meet Jackson Hole postcard. You two have a lot in common. You should hang out together! Here, let me put you in the same drawer."

I was organizing, and I was liking it. And though I didn't know it at the time, there was no going back. Soon my desk became something more than a rectangular pile of my treasures. It became a treasure, too. A monument to organization and efficiency; when I was done I had everything at my fingertips! Need to find that Cracked Magazine with the Jaws cover- no problem! This drawer right here!

I transitioned out of that desk a couple of years later. But believe me, the next one was just as organized. And the next. And the one after that, and so on. But that desk gave off a magical aura that soon subsumed my room, closet, backpack, binders, school locker, and . . . by and by . . . my mind.

That was the nurture moment for my organized nature. It was not my mother's intent (she just wanted me to clean my desk . . . and come out on top of our power struggle), but that incident was pivotal in how I ended up this way. Which brings me to that second question- why does it matter how organized I am? I think I amply covered the advantages in terms of not losing stuff and knowing where things are, as well as the pluses of good time management (no missed meetings for this guy!). But the biggest way I benefit from organization is how I think.

I'm certain that the desk incident helped me to be a more systematic thinker. Prioritizing and categorizing my treasures taught me now to prioritize and categorize my thoughts. I went from being a good student to an exceptional student. I excelled at the kind of logical reasoning that is needed for math, as well as for building an argument about a piece of literature. I did well with long-term projects. I debated in high school. And I've been a writer my whole life.

I also became a psychologist along the way. My sophomore year in college I became fascinated by cognition and development. I later earned a doctorate in school psychology. Now my specialty is learning and a big part of what I do is help struggling students by uncovering breakdown points in the mental abilities that underlie reading, writing, and math. This uncovering is akin to detective work. I have to gather a ton of information (clues, really) and then sort them to discern for patterns. I'm effective and efficient at this because I am organized in my thinking. I know how to sort seemingly disparate data points so that themes emerge. This also helps me to explain test results in ways that lay people, including children, can understand.

Several years ago I developed an assessment findings grid that supports my thinking, actually by externalizing what happens in my head so that I can see it (usually on my impeccable desk). Just as I went through that pile of treasures, deciding what to set aside and how to categorize the rest, I routinely go through piles of assessment findings, sifting and sorting until I can make sense of it all.

So there you have it. I'm a highly organized guy- partly because of my DNA, but also because my mom held firm to her threat of dumping the contents of my desk for non-compliance. I like being organized. It doesn't stress me out and I rarely push my tendencies on others (feel free to reality-check that with my wife). And being organized has helped me help a lot of students who are miserable about their school performance.

Plus I can find my power stapler whenever I need it.

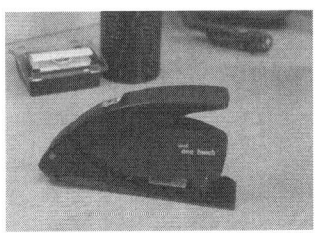

A Little About Craig:

Craig is a neurodevelopmental psychologist who has helped thousands of struggling learners. He has written several books, including "How Can My Kid Succeed in School," which helps parents and educators understand and help students with learning challenges. He considers himself a very balanced person. Meaning he likes both Elvis and the Beatles, Star Wars and Star Trek, and North Carolina and Duke (that's a long story).

I'd Rather Pee Myself

Mara Teal

In order for you to fully grasp the gravity of my story, I have to give you some background.

First, I hate embarrassment. I hate feeling personally embarrassed, and I hate watching other people experience embarrassment. Even when I'm alone (at the age of 27) watching a fictional character on TV in a humiliating situation, I change the channel and keep flipping back to the show until that scene is over. And this is nothing new. While watching movies with my family as a kid, I would (and still do...) conveniently become hungry, or need to use the bathroom (irony to come) when an uncomfortable scene popped up on the screen. I just can't handle it.

Second, as an adolescent, I had this really weird habit of not using the bathroom while I was at school. I can't explain why. It wasn't as if I had performance anxiety, or that the bathrooms were disgusting; I just never used them. I can remember on multiple occasions coming home, racing to the side door of the house, scrambling to get the key into the doorknob, squeezing my legs together, and practically falling over myself to get to the closest bathroom. There were several close calls...and one perfect storm.

One final note: During this time in my life, I babysat a few afternoons a week after school for our next-door neighbors. I loved this family. The mom was/is possibly one of the most genuinely sweet people I've ever met, not to mention beautiful and crazy intelligent. The father I didn't see as much, since he was busy saving people's lives as one of the few medical specialists of his kind. And their baby. Obviously adorable. I, on the other hand, was pretty awkward with pimples in full force.

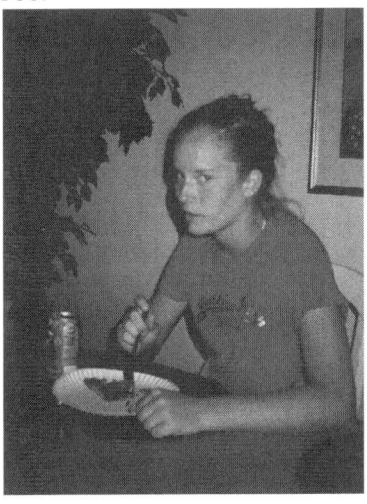

On one particular day of babysitting, the mother of the eight-month old infant was working from home. While she was busy downstairs, I was upstairs watching the baby. I had only been there for maybe 30 minutes when the urge to pee hit, as tends to happen when you have been holding it in for longer than eight hours. I quickly finished changing the baby's diaper, and put her on the floor. I walked into the adjoining bathroom and looked at the toilet. It was baby proofed with a strange looking device. I made several unsuccessful attempts to lift the lever, as my bladder grew more and more pressured. I started to sweat. I took a break, pacing in the bathroom, checking on the baby who was safely crawling around in her room. I returned to the toilet, this time more forceful in my efforts to lift the lid. Nothing worked.

At this point my mind was racing and trying to not think about how relieving it would feel to just let go. I racked my brain for an alternate plan, and clenched my legs together like I'd been using a Thigh Master for years. Then, logically, I thought, "I could pee in the bathtub...or in the sink?" Luckily, rational thought saved me as I realized that standing on the sink to pee would be really difficult to do without falling off, and then I'd have to clean the sink or the bathtub if I were to pee in those spots...and let's be honest, who wants to do that?

I'm sure by now you're all thinking, "This girl's an idiot. Why didn't she just ask the mom, who was down stairs, how to release the lever?" First of all, I agree with you, I was an idiot. Second, I seriously don't think that solution ever occurred to me. And the only reason I can surmise as to why it didn't is because I was EMBARRASSED to admit that I couldn't figure it out. I mean, how humiliating to ask someone for help with a piece of equipment I have never seen before, and was never instructed on how to use, right? That would be catastrophic.

With conflicting thoughts, I frantically moved around the room in no particular order, like I'm Monica Gellar and no one's using coasters. And then it happened...I couldn't hold it any longer. No amount or speed of pacing could hold it at bay. The dam broke...all over myself and the tiled floor. So there I was, standing in my own pee, freaking out, when the baby began slowly crawling towards me. I stretched my arms out, as far away from my soaked-self as possible, picked her up and placed her at the greatest distance from the liquid that I could. She kept trying to come back to me, and as I continued to displace her, I realized that I was screwed. There was no way to conceal it. I was in freaking khaki pants; no one can hide a huge wet spot on that fashionable trend. I was in my worst nightmare; the mom was going to find out that I just urinated all over her bathroom floor. What would she think? Who would she tell? How could I face her?

I picked up the baby because by this time my arms were tired from playing conveyor belt with a 20-something pound sack of potatoes, and conceded. I had to tell her; I couldn't recover. Walking to the banister, I called down to the mom. And just in case there was a chance I might escape with a little bit of dignity, I began to cry. She came to the bottom of the stairs, and looked at me with a sympathetic face, seeing my red cheeks. I began: "Um…so…I really had to go to the bathroom, and I couldn't get the lock off…and…I couldn't hold it anymore…and…." I trailed off; I couldn't say it out loud. I have no idea what the mom said in response; I think I dissociated at this point. All I can remember next is sprinting across their front lawn into my own front yard, and wrenching open the side door as fast as I could, praising God that no one was home to discover they're related to someone who pees themselves at 15 years old. Alone with my shame while changing my soaked bottom half, I took some deep breaths as I came back to reality. That. Just. Happened.

But my shift wasn't over; I had to go back. So I took my proverbial walk of shame, and returned to the neighbors' house. The gorgeous mom opened the door, and immediately began to console me, saying that when she was in residency she got used to cleaning up bodily fluids...and that she had just cleaned up mine. Mortified.

How does someone bounce back from such humiliation, you ask? Deny, repress, and don't speak of it for years. Never happened. That's what I advise all my clients (Sarcasm, for those of you who don't know me). Thankfully the mom seems to have used the same technique, otherwise how could you reason that she, a reputable psychiatrist, would ever refer clients to me?

A Little About Mara:

Mara Teal is a native Charlottean, married a Northerner, loves Boxers (the dog), and can quote the movie My Best Friends Wedding in its near entirety. She was also in a band one time. Mara enjoys working with adolescent and adult females; her specific areas of interest include disordered eating, identity development, self-esteem, relationships, and sexual issues (affairs, addictions, and more).

Rescued

Frank W. Gaskill

I never had any friends later on like the ones I had when I was twelve.
Jesus, does anyone? - Stephen King, "Stand By Me"

I am the only child of an only child who lived through
the Great Depression. Only children tend to be attention hogs
and also socialize more with adult friends of their parents.
I was no exception to this rule. For a variety of reasons both
of my parents were very protective. And yet I was not exposed to a great deal of risk. Due to my Dad's job, I lived in
Esfahan, Iran from 1975 until the revolution of 1979. I would
say that's kind of a big risk. A dichotomy in my life existed
between shelter and exposure to danger. My family and I
would go up onto the roof of our home in Iran and watch the
crowds stream past and scream, "Yankee go home!" I felt absolutely no fear observing these crowds, feeling their threats
against our family and country. And yet I was unable to complete the normal childhood ritual of the sleepover. I could not
successfully sleep over at a friend's house without crying like
a lunatic to go home.

As best as I can remember, my very first sleepover was
at my cousin Billy's house. We were about the same age, and
importantly we were family. I should not have been afraid. I
remember arriving at their house, eating dinner, and having

a vague, anxious feeling build deep within my stomach. I wasn't exactly sure what I was feeling, but all my mind would say is, "You need to be home now!"

As an eight-year-old, I was a science fiction geek and obsessed with aliens. An NBC television show I never failed to miss was called, "Project Blue Book." A precursor to the X-Files, the show was all about stories and sightings of un-identified flying objects and alien abductions.

Lying on the floor of my cousin's family room, I can still vividly see my sci-fi TV show. On that particular episode, a U.F.O. landed in the woods near a home near a forest not un-like the forest near the home in which I was currently having a sleep over (cue music). A mother on the show was wash-ing dishes and steam was rising from the sink fogging the window looking out upon the forest. As she peered through the steam into the yard beyond, blue, glowing aliens walked toward her window. The mother screamed. And I did too. For some dumb reason, or an effort to escape the terror of the

T.V., I decided to get up get a glass of water from the kitchen. Turning the faucet to fill my glass, I of course could not resist the urge to look out of my cousin's kitchen window, and of course I was certain I saw blue aliens walking out of the woods toward me. I lost it. I literally lost it.

Crying uncontrollably I needed to call home by any means necessary. Didn't imagine those aliens. I saw them! I needed to be picked up immediately or else face the probing of the blue aliens. I did not want to be probed! I vaguely recall Aunt Kathy trying to talk me down off the ledge, but I would have none of it. I cried and cried on the phone begging, no...demanding my mom drive 40 minutes to come pick me up late that night. Being the ever vigilant mother of an only child, she did pick me up. I had been rescued. But that was one long, quiet drive home.

After my summer vacation with my cousin, I was again back in pre-Revolutionary war Iran. I had a friend who lived three doors down from my house. And by house, don't imagine typical homes but imagine concrete bunker townhomes set very close to one another. Door-to-door, our houses could not have been more than 70 feet away. And so, the day arrived in which I was graciously asked to spend the night with my friend from three doors down.

My mom and dad sat me down and talked over whether or not they felt I could make it through the night without freaking out. I assured them that I could. My dad emphasized it was very important I stay at my friend's house all night as the city in which we resided was under a dawn to dusk military curfew. Americans were ordered by the embassy to stay in their homes during the curfew. Tensions were high in our city and military vehicles were everywhere. This was essentially a month before the overthrow of the Shah of Iran. With my parents convinced, I headed the approximately 70 feet down the gravel road to my friend's house, stuffed animals in tow. I was in the 4th grade.

And what a great sleepover that was! My friend was a rather privileged kid and was the only individual I knew who owned the very first video game, Pong. His basement was filled with Japanese robots, amazing hot wheels, and about every toy you can possibly imagine. His house was essentially a Disney World just three doors down. Not only were the toys awesome, but his bedroom was built to resemble the moon. He had a replica Apollo space capsule as a bed and it was enormous. We imagined going to the moon and having crazy space wars all evening.

But then the inevitable happened. His mom walked in and said with a clapping of her hands, "Boys, it's time to get to sleep." As the words escaped her mouth, my nervous system collapsed. I was immediately under attack by some unknown threat. I freaked out just as I promised I wouldn't.

Again frantic, I convinced the family to allow me to call my mom and dad. No amount of embarrassment or slobbery crying snot expelled in front of my friend could have stopped my emotional collapse. I had to get home. My parents on the other end of the line really tried to lay down the law with me. They said I needed to sleep through the evening, and they would see me in the morning. Literally, our homes were so close they probably could've just yelled through the walls, and I would've heard them. But I needed to get home.

I still remember that walk of shame as my friend's

father walked me to their stairs watching for my dad to walk out of our stairs. They both looked around to make sure the coast was clear and that no police or military were present. The father of my friend looked at me and softly whispered, "Run!" In a moment I was back home. The disappointing looks and the frustration from my parents paled in comparison to the fear I felt from being too far from home. The next day, I was mortified. I felt like a failure. There would be no way for me to continue my friendship with my neighbor nor be able to go on a sleepover like every other kid. I failed yet again.

And so it was. From the fifth grade until midway through the eighth grade, I never really tried a sleepover again. It helped somewhat that I actually had no friends from the fourth grade until eighth grade. My friends were my stuffed animals, television shows, and building plastic models. Eventually I stopped thinking about sleepovers or that such things were possible. My social life was comprised of visiting with my parents' friends and attempting to monopolize the conversations as much as possible. I learned the definition of the word, "monopolize" early on as my parents would often say, "Frank, you're monopolizing the conversation." I didn't really understand the definition but eventually and shamefully got it.

So why didn't I have friends growing up? My parents, with their vast wisdom and desire for me to have an excellent education, enrolled me in private schools. In my experience, private schools tend to be the deeper end of the social ocean. That may be an unfair stereotype, but I'm going to go with it anyway. When you pair an under socialized kid who's obsessed with science fiction and whose most common conversational partner is a professor in their 40's, the outcome is unlikely to be successful. I was the nerdy, talkative, socially clueless kid surrounded by socially skilled and worldly versed peers. While I liked the Dallas Cowboys, I really did not understand the game. Therefore, by the time I finished my seventh grade year, my parents decided it was time to make a change. I was to leave the bully ridden and supposedly nurturing confines of the private school and learn to find my way in the jungles of public school.

To further emphasize the dichotomy between being protected by my parents and yet exposed to danger, the school I was to attend was incredibly run down and portions were actually condemned. Our auditorium was literally condemned, and yet we continued to hold meetings there each week. Gangs were in the playground, and kids were often held at knife point in the stairwells for their lunch money. This is not an exaggeration. My science teacher actually sent me to the office for yawning, and upon my return to class, she had eaten the lunch I had left there by mistake. I was terrified.

And yet it was within this scary school that my long and seemingly endless drought of friendless nights came to an abrupt end. The salvation for my loneliness came in the form of Trae Shepard. In the first class of my first day of public school, Trae turned in his seat, stuck out his hand, and said, "Hi! My name's Trae. What's your name?" His social skills were excellent. He asked open ended questions and genuinely wanted to get to know me. He was also interested in Dungeons & Dragons which comforted me in thinking "...at least I'm not the only person on Earth who loves this game."

In hindsight, Trae was what people call a connector. He wasn't in one particular grouping of kids but was pretty much well-liked by everyone. He could socialize with basically anybody, was athletic, and also was an amazing artist. He introduced me to a variety of kids and remembering not to "monopolize the conversation," I attempted to lay low and reinvent myself. Things went rather well that fall of eighth grade, and I was able to actually say I had many friends. During that time, I was asked to spend the night with several kids, but due to my anxiety and fear, I always declined making up some lame excuse like, "Sorry, I um...have a piano recital I have to practice for."

I told you it was lame.

I doubt it was conscious on their part but eventually Trae and another buddy Larry suggested they come to my house for a sleepover. I'm pretty sure they recognized my somewhat sheltered existence and laughed when I said my parents would need to meet their parents before they could come over. It was as if I was the girl and my parents needed to meet the guy who is asking their daughter out. Fairly humiliating at the time, but I lived through it.

The night of the sleepover arrived. I was beyond excited and had a nice evening planned of watching movies and playing video games on my Atari. I had popcorn and snacks all prepared including a well thought out Dungeons & Dragons map. This would be the most epic of sleepovers anyone ever had! I was actually correct but not in the way I had planned.

My friends arrived with their parents. They came in and greeted my parents with a firm and polite handshake. Larry leaned over and whispered, "On my signal we head to your room." He added, "Don't ask any questions and just do what we say." Now I was excited but also terrified. Had I misjudged these kids? Was I going to do something that would break rules? What about all the work I put into our exciting night of activities? What was happening?

At some unknown signal, my friends politely excused us to get "unpacked" for the sleepover. As soon as we got into my bedroom, Larry shut the door behind us. He said in a rather forceful, quiet tone, "Don't say a word. Do everything we say." Trae and Larry unzipped their duffel bags dumping a ridiculously large number of knives, camouflage clothing, face paint, duct tape, and five or six BB and pellet guns. I couldn't breathe and had no idea what to say or do. Trae said, "Hide this quick!" And so I did. We shoved the items under my bed, on the high shelves in my closet, and anywhere else I could stuff the evidence of whatever was about to happen that night.

Surprisingly, the rest of the evening went exactly as I

had planned. We were having a blast watching MTV, playing video games, stuffing our faces with candy and pizza. My parents came in around 10:30 PM and said, "Don't you boys stay up too late tonight." We of course said that we would go to bed at a reasonable hour and had our sleeping bags all prepared in front of the television. I figured we would just fall asleep out there eventually.

As my parents headed off to bed, Larry asked me an important question, "Do you know the alarm code to your alarm system?" Well of course I did but why on earth did he ask me that question. He reiterated his earlier warning to me stating, "For the rest of the night you need to do exactly what we say and everything will go fine. Tonight we are going to have some serious fun!" As he stated this, he was stuffing clothing and pillows into our sleeping bags trying to make it look like fake teenagers were sound asleep watching MTV.

For the next five hours I took more risks than I had in my entire life. My two best friends (yes, I actually had best friends now for the first time ever) quietly unlocked the back door to our patio. There was a 7 foot wall which we then scaled giving us access to 1 mile of unlit roads surrounded by swamps and countless snakes. We had already strapped on all of our pellet guns, and I had two knives duct taped to my legs. My face was blacked out with camouflage face paint. In that moment I was awesome! I felt on fire with excitement. And so we discussed our plans for the evening. We knew that there was a potential girl sleepover in the more wealthy section of my hometown, and we also had heard rumors that there was a senior high football team party going on somewhere in town. On and on we walked into the dark plotting our evening.

My buddies and I walked about 5 miles in the middle of the night to make it to the girls' party. I recently checked Google maps to make sure that this mileage was not an exaggeration of youthful memories. That distance was dead on. Teenager hormones will take you just about anywhere especially after midnight. By the time we reached the girl's house, all the lights were off. The party was over. Time for Plan B.

Retracing our path back toward my house we explored a different section of my town. Late at night, sound travels. We heard the music coming from the football party. We commenced recon. Crawling through ditches filled with red clay mud, our jeans were soaked and stained. Like brave soldiers would, we crawled through trenches of water and sewer drains appearing near the backyard of the rumored senior football party. Van Halen was blasting through the night with kids drinking and having a blast. So what better idea would it be than to train a high-powered, scope-mounted pellet gun onto one of the football player's butt cheeks? And that's exactly what Larry did that night.

Larry's shot was true and found its mark. There was an audible pause in the partying as somebody yelled out. In my excitement and utter fear, I snapped a branch, and all eyes turned toward the darkness where the shot was fired and we were hidden. Larry yelled, "Run!" And so we did.

We ran and ran and ran into the darkness. Close to the road leading home, a car filled with really big 18-year-olds stopped us. They asked us where we were going and implicated us in a recent shooting at their party. Clearly these were not the most intelligent individuals on the planet. They were looking at us as we were strapped down with pellet guns, BB pistols, camouflage paint, and knives duct taped to every part of us that we could find. And they were still not clear that we were the actual shooters. Really?? There's a phrase called, "Occam's razor," which basically means if it looks like a duck and quacks like a duck, then it must be a duck. The simplest solution is most often the answer. Despite the obvious data, I could sense they still were not clear we were not the shooters. That's when I pulled my trump card.

Now that I actually had a circle of friends and my connector was Trae Shepard, I called upon my unlikely connection and also lifelong best friend in Scott Vermillion. Scott was in my grade ultimately becoming the quarterback of our high school football team. His brother had reached "Studom" earlier that year on the high school football team, later going on to be a wide receiver at the University of North Carolina at Chapel Hill. He was also a calendar boy for his fraternity's fundraiser and was basically the stud of the day.

I don't know if it was all my conversations with adults, but my negotiation and "monopolizing" skills kicked in. I recognized that one of the high school kids interrogating us was also on the football team. I ingratiated myself with him stating that I was a big fan of his skills. I also said that I went to every football game and that my best friend was Scott Vermillion. I asked him if he knew who Tom Vermillion was. I believe he may have been the captain of the team at that time and upon speaking his name, I saw this individual visibly shrink back. I reiterated that my friends and I had been just running around in the dark, and there was no way we could have been that close to whatever party they were having. We were miles away and we could not have been the shooters. I said that I hoped they had a good night but that we had to run home because we were out way past our bedtime. The guys laughed and gave me a high five. I told them to be sure to say hi to Tom for me and that I was certain he would vouch for me.

We walked back to my house in silence. We felt we had come close to death. But there was a greater death awaiting me at home. So many nightmares raced through my mind of walking into the home with all the lights on and my mom smoking her cigarette and drumming her fingers. Walking in fear and relief, we made it back home and scaled the wall to my home. I climbed into my sleeping bag but not before I took off my jeans, turned them inside out, and put them in the laundry hamper. They were still covered in mud from my crawling through the trenches but turning them inside out would hide the evidence for sure. The jeans would get washed, and everything would be fine. Into our sleeping bags we went falling asleep to music videos played on MTV circa 1983.

Late the next morning, we awoke to more music videos, but still barely teenagers, we turned to Bugs Bunny and Roadrunner. We were still kids despite our adult adventure from the night before. There in my den, side-by-side, we were still kids. With pressure from my peers and risks I had never taken, I was welcomed into the world of being a teenager by true friends. We began to laugh a little bit without even speaking. That is until I heard my mom yell in a crackling voice, "Frank, get in here!" My buddies shot me a quick, startled look. I took a long, slow walk to greet my mom with her drumming fingers and cigarette. Unexpectedly, she was holding up a muddy pair of jeans.

"Where did this mud come from?" My mom inquired in an annoyed fashion.

"The yard," I fumbled having no idea what my mouth would say next.

"We don't have this kind of mud in our yard," my mom replied.

"Sure we do. I was walking the dog last night late and I kind of fell down. We have that kind of mud."

My mom replied, "It's time for your friends to go."

And with that statement, my friends stayed throughout high school and on into middle-age. I had many sleepovers after that night. The sleepovers were filled with Dungeons & Dragons, nerdy movies, and not a single girl party. My parents had the best intentions and understandably wanted to keep their only duckling safe and secure. They did their absolute best, and I am grateful for that.

And... I am grateful for the best of friends who showed me what it meant to live and take risks and live outside of fear. In the end, my friends rescued me. They will always Stand By Me.

A Little About Frank:

Having only recently been able to use public restrooms with the help of his iPhone, Dr. Gaskill a.k.a. "Dr. G" is the resident clinically insane person at Southeast Psych. He more or less impersonates a psychologist and is also a contributor to the ShrinkTank podcast as, "The Psych Weasel." Dr. Gaskill actually specializes in Asperger's, effective parenting, and how technology and kids can interface successfully. He is a founding partner at Southeast Psych, one of the largest psychology practices in the United States. Gaskill is also the co-author of Max Gamer (2011, Hero House Publishing), a graphic novel about Asperger's. Drawing on his years of experience in private practice, Gaskill is also focused on his book, How We Built Our Dream Practice: Innovative Ideas for Building Yours which he co-authored with Dr. David Verhaagen.

THE RISE AND FALL OF SAD SAM

KRISTIN DALEY

Through much of my childhood, I was made to feel that my body was something of which I should be ashamed. There were the taunts by family members; my father pointing out that he was worried I would die of diabetes if my weight didn't come down and my brothers heckled me constantly. These were followed by the even louder taunts by classmates and random kids on the street. I can remember walking my neighbor's dog past a group of teenage guys playing basketball and one of the kids stated , "I wonder which one's the dog?" My body was a deficit, and I tried to use intellect and wit to gain positive peer reactions.

Around the age of 15, I went through a growth spurt in which my body weight evened out. I was a competitive swimmer, so my body shape responded well to this growth spurt. I found myself in this weird place of being viewed as being physically attractive. We had just moved to a new city, and it was even stranger to have people know the new, attractive version, rather than the uncomfortable, awkward body. I realized that clothes looked good on my body, and my mom backed off from her disparaging comments and comparisons between my body and houses. I actually had a friend who was worried that I was too skinny.

The summer after I turned 16, I decided to trade swimming for smoking, and my weight took an additional nose-dive. It felt powerful, and I was gaining a lot of male attention. I took to wearing very tight clothes, because I could, and started to use the male attention to gain social status and something I had never really had much of in the past- friends.

The downside of wearing all of the tight clothes was that they highlighted an unfortunate figure flaw that is experienced by many teenage girls and women- one of my breasts was larger than the other. My boyfriend would laugh at this characteristic, and I started to keep track of the clothing that made it more or less obvious. I vacillated between loose t-shirts (cover the flaw!) and tight tops (attract the boys!). It was a pretty pathetic period. I came up with a name for the larger, sadder breast- Sad Sam. He seemed to look downward, while the other one seemed to be happy and look straight ahead.

One day, it occurred to me that the best way to help Sad Sam was to try to make him more attractive. I knew that my parents would never go for corrective surgery; they had opted out of a much-needed tonsillectomy when I was eight because it was an inconvenience to them. I had to figure out how to beautify him by the means that were accessible to me. I started with sizing things to best match him. I discovered my favorite shirt, the looser, deep V-neck, which highlighted my "assets" without highlighting Sad Sam. I also started to think about the best way to beautify him, and decided that a tattoo was the way to go. My boyfriend at the time decided he wanted to get a tattoo across his shoulder blades, and knew of a studio that was good, yet also willing to overlook the fact that we were not 18. I had chosen an Egyptian eye pattern, called the Eye of Horace, because it was supposed to be symbol of protection. It also seemed like an appropriate fit for a breast tattoo because breasts tend to remind me of eyeballs in a weird way. I viewed this as a positive symbol and decided that placing it on the lower part of my breast would accomplish two goals- I would beautify Sad Sam, and I would also never have to worry about the tattoo being seen in one of my revealing V-necks.

On one fateful summer day, we made the long drive to downtown Gastonia for our tattoo sessions. The tattoo artist, Randy, was a very large man, about 350 pounds, and covered in tattoos, which was to be expected but still felt a little shocking to me. He decided that I should go first, because it was such a small tattoo, and the cost was $40. I think that it took all of five minutes for him to do, but his wife and son visited him while he was working on it. I had never been super shy about my body, but there was an added feeling of ick when this ugly dude and his whole family were evaluating his work on my breast. I then waited several hours for my boyfriend to get his tattoo done, which happened to be a very large logo for a company that was pretty obscure but has since become very famous. Without his shirt on, this guy is a walking billboard.

When we got home, I was dying to show it to anyone that I could. I was proud of my new body art and even showed it to my mother who promptly called the police to report the under age tattoo job. Word got around school about our tattoo adventure, and I was even interviewed by my school paper about having gone through such a permanent body modification (this was the early 90's and these things were still pretty rare). I informed them there was no chance I would ever be embarrassed about tattoos, and figured that my grandchildren would assume I was the coolest grandmother. During my senior year of high school, I followed through with my plan to add to the canvas on my body and got a sun across my lower back. I had seen a tattoo like this when I was on tour with the Grateful Dead during the prior summer and thought it was the ultimate in beauty. I could not afford what a professional artist would charge for such a large tattoo, so I went the economical route. My friend Joey wanted to be a tattoo artist and had fashioned his own tattoo gun from an ink pen and all sort of other random parts. He offered to draw it and place it on my back for free. It took hours and was quite painful, but I was thrilled with the outcome. The ink started to bleed out as the tattoo healed, but the initial product was BEAUTIFUL to my friends and me.

I had kept this tattoo a secret from my parents because of their strong negative reaction to the first one. My brothers thought I was an absolute moron to have such a large tattoo done by a novice, missing the genius of the bargain that I had gotten. The secret from my parents lasted until Easter that spring, when I awoke to my father screaming, "What the hell is that on your back?" He had come to wake me for church, and my shirt had ridden up while I was sleeping. I can't say it was the first time that I surprised him in an awful way, nor was it the last.

After a year or two, the tattoo grew increasing splotchy and closer to resembling a prison tattoo. At the ripe old age of 21, I had it redone by another artist friend learning to tattoo, but this one had a real tattoo gun. I was getting wiser, for sure. He drew up an abstract design of a sun, which would cover the original sun, and we decided to aim for a little more area of the back, simply to make it proportionate. He worked on it for hours, over a couple of sessions, and did not spare the ink, just to be sure that it would be covered well. Thanks to his inexperience, it was painful, and took a long time to heal. Once again, ink seemed to bleed out with the healing process and I was left with a few pale blotches in these huge stretches of black. I consulted with a professional tattoo artist to find out what could be done to help it. The look of horror and amusement on his face pretty much said it all- I had gone way too far and there was no salvaging it. He said that people with fair skin can have a hard time with solid black tattoos, and he did not think that there would be a way to make the color consistent across my whole back. He recommended removal, which would be painful and expensive. Around that time, the terms "asshat" and "tramp stamp" also started to enter the zeitgeist.

Over the years, I had forgot about Sad Sam and his adornment. My husband used to laugh that all it took was a few drinks and I would gladly show my tattoos to anyone who was interested, but this changed as I grew up and developed more of a frontal lobe. My breasts served their intended function of nursing babies, and I stopped really thinking about how they appeared in shirts. I considered it a positive thing that normal clothing could cover all of my big mistakes. I was restricted in swimsuit selection, but what woman isn't? After many years, I found myself working as a professional, and working out at a popular gym most mornings before work. I started to feel really embarrassed about having to change in the locker room, because I knew that my large back tattoo would likely change people's impression of me, should they catch a glimpse of it. I contacted a tattoo removal practice, and went in for my first session. Laser tattoo removal is the most painful thing that I have ever endured, and I have given birth to a ten-pound baby without pain medication. The sessions are about 20 minutes long, and I have been through 5, but I still have a long way to go. My doctor broke down and prescribed me some anxiety and pain medicine to help me make it through the rest of the process, but I still can't bring myself to schedule another session. So, needless to say, my back tattoo looks amazing.

About two days before my 40th birthday, I had an annual check-up. During the exam, my doctor found a lump in my breast, and told me that I needed to have an extensive mammogram to make sure everything was okay. We went out of town for my birthday, and I fielded reminder calls and appointment confirmation calls from the radiology practice. Apparently, they felt it was a big deal that I keep the appointment. I joked with my husband that I might finally be able to get surgery on Sad Sam to make him match up with his buddy and we tried to keep things jovial about the whole evaluation. I see several clients who are coping with breast cancer and had to put that reality into the back of my brain.

The day of the big mammogram finally came and I went in for the appointment. My radiology tech was very upbeat, and told me all about her life, her experience with breast cancer, and let me know that almost every lump is benign. We laughed about the fact that I thought a lump would be this big protruding thing and was pretty surprised by how flat my lump really was. The tech told me that most mammograms are several pictures. My doctor had scheduled me for an ultrasound in addition to the mammogram, but she shrugged it off as very unlikely to be performed. She took the initial images, cracking jokes and very casual the whole time; it was a pretty bizarre experience on my end but I appreciated her tendency to keep things light. She then looked at the images, made a lot of "hmms" and "huhs," and then told me that they would actually have to take a few additional images. She proceeded to take several other images, with my body contorted in all sorts of odd angles; there were some painful moments. She invited me to come and look at the images, stating that breast cancer appears to be white on the image; just before showing me an image of my breast that was almost solid white. She blanched a little and stated that it was unlikely that all of that white was actually cancer, but more than likely just some unusual tissue. She said she would discuss it with the radiologist, but was sure that we would not need to do the ultrasound. Right before she left the room, she ducked her head back and asked, "Will you have to go back to work today?"

Images ran through my head. My client schedule for one, would I have to see any of my clients with breast cancer on the day that I found out that I had breast cancer? How would I keep it together? Would this be a really big deal or just a moderately big deal? A blogger who had breast cancer had just died, and she had seemed younger and more vibrant than me, prior to her diagnosis. I also had a few acquaintances that had been through breast cancer treatment, and they had seemed pretty okay. I decided that I would stick with my initial idea that this would be a ticket to breast reconstruction, rather than a major health threat.

The tech came back into the room, and told me that, just to be on the safe side, they would like to perform the ultrasound and measure the density of the tissue. I joked that I had never had an ultrasound where there wasn't a baby on the other end, so I hoped that we didn't find a baby in my breast. She no longer seemed jovial and I started to feel a little panicky. She had me lay down in a very contorted

position, so that she could get the right angle on Sad Sam.
As I lay down in this odd position, she gasped. "You have the
most awful bruise! I can't believe I hurt you so badly with the
mammogram!" She asked if I was in a lot of pain, and also
questioned if I was taking any blood-thinners. I informed her
that I was not really in any pain, and also not taking any med-
ications. She persisted, asking about aspirin or anything that
I might not realize was a blood-thinning medication. I kept
wishing she would focus on this ultrasound- we could worry
about this bruise later. I needed to know if I had cancer or
not. She went and got her nurse manager, and they started
to write the incident report. They explained that I would
need to keep my breast on ice for the rest of the day, and
they hoped that this would not disrupt my clinical schedule
too much, but it was very important that I care well for the
bruise. I informed them that I was sure that my clients would
definitely not notice that I had an ice pack on my breast and
asked if we could please proceed with the ultrasound. The
tech was now absolutely quiet as she measured and made
notes. She told me that she would be back with the radiologist shortly, and wanted me to remain in my contorted
position until he came, because he would want to look at it
himself. The doctor came in, a kind older man, and remarked
about my awful bruise. The tech informed him that the incident report had already been written, and they had given me
instructions on wound care. The doctor informed me that
all was fine- there was a lot of dense tissue but nothing that
appeared to be cancerous. He stated that I should keep up
annual appointments, and we would go from there. I exhaled,
for the first time in about 20 minutes, and he left the room.

As I sat up, the tech came in with her ice pack and went through the bruise care instructions yet again. She kept pointing to the worrisome spot on my breast, and all I could see was my Eye of Horace decoration for poor Sad Sam. It occurred to me that I wasn't seeing a bruise anywhere, just my tattoo. "Is this what you are talking about?" I asked, indicating my tattoo. "Yes, it is just awful," stated the tech. I let her know that it was actually a tattoo, admittedly a 24 year-old tattoo in an odd position. She put on her glasses and regarded it closely, and then started to giggle. "Well," she said, "I feel better to know that I didn't do that to you!" She left the room and I got dressed. As I walked out of the office, giggles from the nursing stations rippled out with me- this was definitely the joke of the year for this practice. I was just grateful to not have cancer and not have to spend the rest of the day with my breast on ice. After all of those years of attention, a clean bill of health was really all that was needed to make Sad Sam a lot less sad.

A LITTLE ABOUT KRISTIN:

Kristin Lamb Daley was born in Hanover, PA, the middle child in her family. They moved several times through her upbringing, and eventually landed in Charlotte, NC, where she has stuck. She briefly escaped Charlotte to attend UNC-Chapel Hill, and remains a Carolina girl through and through. She had long dreamed of being a doctor, so much so that her family used to refer to her as "Dr. Lamb." She started a career in sleep and psychology, and eventually received her doctorate in health psychology from UNC-Charlotte. She still daydreams of attending medical school, possibly after her own children get through school, and insists that people call her Dr. Daley whenever possible.

Dillon & Ellen

Dave Verhaagen

My wife, Ellen, was born to American parents in Germany on a military base. She lived in Iran after that for a few years, then moved to an Army town in Texas. Most of her formative years, though, were spent in the mountains of North Carolina. You'd think growing up in a rural town with horses and cows in your neighbor's front yard would mean she was comfortable with animals, but Ellen's family never had a pet. Not a cat. Not a bird. Not a gerbil or a hamster. Not even a dog.

I, on the other hand, always had a dog in the house. When I was very young we got a weird dog who made me sneeze a lot and once jumped up and bit my face for no good reason, leaving a scar near my jawline that I have to this day. Needless to say, that dog didn't last too long. After that, though, we had a string of poodles that were as neurotic as they were hypoallergenic.

The first was Shawn, a medium-sized poodle who was the Andy Dufresne of dogs, carefully plotting his Shawshank escape each night. The moment the front door was opened even a crack, Shawn would magically appear and make his prison break, only to return hours later. There was no sense in chasing him, as he was apparently the fastest poodle in the history of the world.

One night, he returned with a limp and a bit of a hump in his back. We found out later that he had been run over by a motorcycle. (How we discovered that, I have no idea. Shawn didn't tell us nor did the motorcycle guy, but somehow we knew.) This slightly curtailed his getaways, but it made him more protective of me and my brother, for some reason. To exploit this new overprotectiveness for his personal amusement, my father would put on several heavy coats and lay us on the ground and act like he was beating us, hitting the floor beside us and growling like a deranged person. Shawn would snarl viciously and attack him and bite the crap out of those coats, like those police dogs you see on the YouTube videos. Even with all those layers of clothing, he would still sometimes clamp down really hard and break the skin on my dad's arm, which made him upset, like somehow the dog should know this was all a big pretend game. Still, my father would do it again every couple of weeks, some-times at our urging, and get his arm punctured about half the time.

While we still had Shawn, we got another poodle, this time a little one named Gigi who may have been the most insane animal every born. Gigi would have false pregnancies every few months where she would (incorrectly) believe she was pregnant, then round up her squeaky toys and put them in my mother's closet and lay on them like she was nursing them for a few weeks at a time. We would hear her in the closet whining for days on end. She was a nut, to say the least.

She was also incredibly spiteful. If we would leave the house for longer than what suited her, she would poop within millimeters of the front door, so when you opened it, it would smear all over the carpet. It was very deliberate. She would poop so close to the door that you couldn't open it even a little bit to determine if she had done it again. We never caught her in the act because she only did it when we were away, but I am certain she had to back herself up until her butt actually touched the door to achieve this level of precision.

For some reason, my parents thought it was a good idea to add a third poodle named Pumpkin to the mix. I remember two things about Pumpkin. First, she had the worst smelling breath imaginable. In fact, after she kicked the bucket, my father said we all knew she was dead because she smelled better. Second, I remember she was incredibly devious, like a dog sociopath. She was able to con the other two dogs into antisocial dog activities on a regular basis with a kind of Charles Manson-esque sway over them.

The most notable example was the night we came home late from visiting relatives. The lights were out, but we immediately could feel the smear under the front door as it opened. Through the faint light coming in the windows, we could also see what looked like snow in the living room and streamers instead of curtains in the windows. It was incomprehensible. There was no slot in any of our brains to make sense of it. My mom turned on the lights and the entire downstairs looked like a Winter Wonderland with fluffy white "snowflakes" floating in the air and covering the entire floor. The curtains had been ripped in long vertical tears.

It took awhile to figure out what had happened, but it soon became clear that the three dogs had ripped open every pillow and cushion they could find and shook them so hard the down filling and stuffing floated through the air. Then Pumpkin had run off the arm of the couch and launched herself into the curtains, grabbing each one as high up as she could with her sharp Poodle teeth. She held on tight as she slid down, shredding the curtain to the ground. She went back and did it again and again and again until all six living room curtains were in complete tatters. And, of course, at some point during all these shenanigans, Gigi went to the front door and pooped again. Our entire family—my mom, dad, brother, and myself—stood in the doorway and beheld this spectacle: poop smeared at the door, white stuffing and feathers covering the floor and floating in the air, shredded curtains.

Despite all this, my parents never stopped having dogs in the house, including two dachshunds who got so fat they couldn't walk, a Great Dane who put my nephew's entire head in his mouth, and a mostly deaf and blind dog who would snap at any attempt to pet her. The dogs varied from awesome to pitiful to deranged.

When Ellen and I got married, I assumed we would get a dog, since this was always the case for me growing up. She assumed the opposite, since she never had a dog in the house and doing so would be bordering on insane. We lived in Philadelphia during our first year of marriage and I recall visiting a friend up there who had a black Lab that decided it wanted to sit right beside Ellen, for reasons unknown. Ellen looked completely terrified, the way the humans in Jurassic Park do when they keep perfectly still so the T-Rex won't eat them. I knew if she was scared of a Labrador retriever, then my dog days were over.

So it was a pretty big surprise for me when she got me a hound dog for my 30th birthday. He was a puppy named Dillon that she had gotten from the pound and he had gigantic paws, which was a clear signal of how big this dog was going to get. If he even came close to growing into those big feet, he was going to be huge. Of course, that's exactly what he did. He grew to be well past 100 lbs. of hound dog.

Dillon turned out to be 98% of a great dog. He was fun and playful. He let our girls, who came along after he had been part of our family for a few years, sit on him and twist his ears and semi-torture him without a hint of complaint. He was a great house protector, frequently surveying the yard and street for potential bad guys, which he often found in the form of: 1) women pushing baby carriages, 2) squirrels, 3) falling leaves.

It was the other 2% that was the issue. The first major event happened one Friday afternoon. I had been at work and Ellen was flying in from Miami where she had spent several days providing corporate computer training. I came home at the end of the day and opened the door. My mouth hung open as I looked at the calamity in front of me. There were four soda cans still in the plastic rings lying on the hardwood floor, but each one had been bitten and had sprayed Diet Coke all over the walls and pictures in the foyer. To my left, the side of my La-Z-Boy recliner had been completely chewed off. Completely. I walked slowly through the house, my head spinning. A trash can had been tipped over and trash was strewn throughout every downstairs room. In the kitchen, a mound of garbage was soaked in urine. And standing right beside this was Dillon wagging his tail. He was overjoyed to see me. Me not so much glad to see him.

I had no idea why he had done any of this, but I chalked it up to him being a bored and lonely dog. I resolved to take him on more walks and play more with him so he wouldn't feel neglected. Not long after that, though, he ratcheted up the reign of terror to the next level. When I came home, he had eaten—eaten!—a two-foot section of the back door, part of the door frame, a sizable section of the wall beside the door, and had crushed the doorknob with his teeth. He had almost succeeded in chewing his way out to the backyard through the wall of the house.

I still had no clue what was happening. Surely this wasn't just because he was bored or lonely. A few weeks later, I had my answer. We were home one evening when a thunderstorm came rumbling up, which is a fairly common occurrence during the summer months in Charlotte, where we had since relocated. At the first hint of thunder, Dillon began to run from room to room in a complete panic and totally out of his mind. He knocked over a tall and expensive lamp, shattering it, then promptly peed on the carpet. Before I could subdue him, he had clawed his way through the back of our entertainment center in a partially-successful attempt to get inside one of its compartments. Once inside, he chewed the TV cable off the wall.

After that, it all began to make more sense. If we were at home with him during one of these storms, he would begin to shake and spin around in circles, so we would immediately grab him and make him sit beside us until the storm passed. It was when we weren't there that the catastrophes happened.

We had our answer, but the solution wasn't as easy as it seemed. As much as we liked him having a run of the whole house, we decided we had to put him in a big steel crate while we were gone for his safety and, frankly, the safety of the house and all of our earthly possessions.

We put the crate in our bedroom against the far wall facing our bed. This seemed like mission accomplished, but the first time we returned after he had been locked in the crate during the thunderstorm, we found that he had slammed the crate forward on the carpeted floor until it reached our bed. He then chewed through a portion of the crate door, pulled the comforter off our king size bed into his crate and had eaten a good amount of it.

I repaired the door and reinforced it with some additional metal. Weeks passed without incident and it seemed like all was well until a thunderstorm came up during the middle of the night and Dillon began slamming into the side of the crate so loudly we were forced to evacuate our bedroom and go into the guest room. To put it in perspective, he was much louder than the thunder booming all around us. Before I left the room, I placed a wooden chair between his crate and our bed so there was zero chance he would ever be able to make it to our bed again.

The next morning, I found that he had chewed through part of the crate door again, then chewed the leg off of the chair, which promptly fell over, giving him direct access to the bed. After he slammed the crate into the bed, he ate the new comforter, another blanket, all the sheets, a pillow, and a dust ruffle. He had also managed to pull the mattress off the box springs and had eaten a corner of the mattress.

By this point, Ellen had decided she had had enough. She was ready to put Dillon in a burlap sack and throw him off a bridge. I protested, but ultimately agreed that we needed to do something. We arrived at a solution: drugs. We got a vet to prescribe a heavy-duty dog tranquilizer that we were to give him any time there was the hint of a storm.

The tranquilizer worked like a charm, maybe too well. Once it kicked in, he would lie on the floor and thick drool would pool around his mouth, and nearly always, one little doo-doo ball would plop out just below his tail. The problem with the tranquilizer was that it took upwards of an hour to work, so we constantly had to check the weather reports and give him the pill as a pre-emptive strike. It was a tricky proposition. We were always one rogue storm away from saying goodbye to the ficus tree or the laundry hamper. And if we were wrong and no storm ever materialized, we were left with a hundred pounds of drooling jelly dog with no bladder or bowel control for the rest of the day.

Still, we eventually got it engineered to the point of near-perfection with a minimal amount of false-positives (drugging him when no storm was coming) or false-negatives (failing to knock him out before a storm arrived, resulting in hundreds of dollars of property damage). However, Ellen was still not a big fan.

"This dog is driving me crazy!" she would frequently say.

I suspected she was secretly buying large burlap sacks and scouting out bridges. I thought for sure I would come home one day to find Dillon had gone to live on a "farm" in a rural part of the state.

We hung in there with Dillon, though, which is probably a good thing because it was unlikely we could have gotten rid of him if we had tried. I developed a theory that the dog was unkillable. I first formed this notion the day I was playing fetch with him after work. He would bring a ball to me and I would throw it to the furthest point in the backyard and he would retrieve it again and again and again, much like most dogs will do, with seemingly boundless energy. I faked him out a few times and he quickly got wise to me, so he started looking back to see if I really had thrown it before he went racing through the yard. When I threw the ball for real, he was still facing me, but began running away at full speed.

"Dillon! Stop!" I yelled. "Stop!"

But it was too late. He ran into a wooden post at full speed and hit his head squarely with a sound much like a bowling ball being dropped onto a wooden floor. The inertia of his gallop slammed the rest of him into the post. I thought for sure he was going to collapse into a heap, but he quickly regained his balance and shook his jowls from side to side like a cartoon character that had been hit in the face with a shovel. He looked back at me, then trotted to the ball and brought it back for me to throw it again. What would have probably killed me and brain-damaged most other mammals barely registered for him.

About a year later, I was in the backyard preparing to bring the trash rollout to the street. I opened the gate and Dillon made a Shawn-worthy jailbreak, charging out at full stride. A car slammed on its brakes and then there was a sickening thump so loud I could hear it plainly from the back of the house. I ran as fast as I could to the front where Dillon was standing in the road in front of our neighbor, Judy Davis' car. She frantically rolled down the window.

"Is that your dog? I'm so sorry! I'm so sorry!" she said. "He just ran out in front of me and I didn't have time to stop."

Dillon looked over at me and wagged his tail. He ran back up into the yard while I consoled Judy.

"It's not your fault, Judy," I said. "He just got out of the gate before I could stop him."

"I'm so sorry," she said again. "Do you need to take him to the vet?"

I looked over at Dillon who was now sitting in the yard, panting a little, but looking otherwise fine.

"I'll take care of him, Judy. Please don't worry about it," I said.

She drove off shaking her head in shock and I let Dillon back inside the house where he promptly jumped up on the coach and wagged his tail. I sat beside him and checked his ribs and legs for any sign of trouble. He didn't wince or seem to have the slightest bit of pain as I pressed my hands along his side. He was clearly just as fine as he was before being hit by a car going 25 mph.

He couldn't be killed.

He could die, though. Dillon lived ten good years until one day he gave out in the middle of the living room. He collapsed on the floor and couldn't get back up. We knew it was time. Ellen and I both drove him to the vet who agreed that it was his day to go to dog heaven.

Ellen cried like a baby. She went from cursing the day she ever got me that dog to being deeply sad on the day he left us. She thought about all the times he was protector of the house and so patient and kind with our girls. She thought about the joy he had and the joy he had brought us. Even the sting of the thousands of dollars of damage he had done to our home had faded and she knew it would all make for a good story, which is a big part of what makes life worth living. Neither of us would ever have thought we would say it, but we were both grateful that we hung in there with him.

We've had three dogs since, including one that is a legitimate candidate for "Dumbest Animal Who Has Ever Lived," the same dog who pees on nearly everything, including chairs, curtains, the gas grill, and the other dog. None of them, though, could ever compare to the great Dillon. I'm certainly a few thousand bucks poorer, but my life is somehow a lot richer.

A Little About Dave:

Dave Verhaagen is a psychologist, author, bad magician, goat herder, gangsta rapper, bionic man, underwear model, crime scene investigator, game show host, circus clown, oil tanker captain, musketeer, horse whisperer, cryptographer, bounty hunter, celebrity impersonator, bail bondsman, puppeteer, manicurist, stock car racer, ventriloquist, dolphin trainer, prime minister, cheese sculptor, leprechaun, scuba instructor, beekeeper, pastry chef, alien abductee, bodyguard, potato peeler, matador, gold prospector, synchronized swimmer, barista, cutlery salesman, wizard, hip-hop dancer, storm chaser, professional wrestler, lounge singer, conquistador, snowman, herpetologist, bubble boy, roustabout, nuclear decontamination technician, cat behavior consultant, lumberjack, husband and father.

"GOLDDIGGER"

JONATHAN HETTERLY

BACKSTORY

My wife agreed to marry me for better or for worse. I take marital vows in the literal sense. I remember early in our engagement I foolishly tried to hold onto that valiant attempt to present the best version of myself to her. But it would not be long before we both saw the true versions of one another, warts and all. I don't think there is a better story that illustrates my wife seeing the true, unvarnished version of me than the story you are about to read. The following incident is 100% true, and not true in the Argo sense or the David Sedaris sense, but 100% accurate and true.

My wife and I have a very unusual backstory. I actually proposed to her before we ever went on a formal date. The majority of our engagement was spent on opposite coasts.

And to add an extra layer of intrigue in the early days of our relationship, we met each other in Branson, Missouri, the Las Vegas for Mormons. Because of the long-distance in our relationship, our engagement lasted one year. But my wife Julie moved to the west coast and was near me in southern California as I finished up my last year of college. She lived 45 minutes away from me in Newport Beach with one of her old college roommates. I was living off campus with three roommates in a two bedroom apartment. For the most part Julie would come up and hang out until we got our own apartment and married.

THE SWALLOWING

One night Julie was over and we were hanging out with my three roommates. We were eating food and watching television when all of a sudden I realized that my back right molar was missing its gold crown. I immediately panicked. I knew I most likely had swallowed it and I had no financial options for replacing that crown. Although I was a full-time assistant manager at Chuck-E-Cheese's with great health benefits, I wasn't sure if I opted for a dental plan. And even if I had done so, I was pretty sure I did not have the extra finances to replace a gold crown. So there I was, just a normal evening hanging out with my roommates and my soon-to-be bride and I just swallowed a gold crown with no way of retrieving it.

MY DENTAL HISTORY

Swallowing my gold crown was just the latest in a long

series of mishaps and misfortunes involving my mouth and my teeth. Truth be told, by that point in my life I probably had over a dozen cavities and had one root canal. I also had an implant tooth as a replacement for one that got shot out by a BB gun when I was in high school. Some friends and I were reenacting the Vietnam conflict, and as the only Asian of the group, I portrayed the entire Vietcong army. In order to embody my character, I wore a stir fry wok on my head as a hat. I am known for committing to my characters and my projects. Prior to this incident, the last major dental procedure I had undergone was getting all of my wisdom teeth pulled out on Christmas Eve my second year of college. I was just about to become a California resident which would get me dropped from my mother's health and dental insurance. So I had to get my wisdom teeth pulled out before the end of the year. Unfortunately, by the time I flew home after the semester finals the only available time for the surgery was Christmas Eve. I remember spending an entire Christmas break groggy on Vicodin, drooling uncontrollably in a haze, while sleeping on a pullout couch in my mom's new apartment. So all of this happened in my life, and yet somehow it escaped my logic that it would be a really good idea to have dental coverage. So there I was with no dental coverage, no money, and no gold crown because I had just swallowed it. And I was a couple months away from getting married, still in college, and not in the greatest financial position. It probably took about 30 seconds of frustration and anger (mostly toward myself, but some directed at that spaghetti I had eaten) before the obvious solution came to my mind. I would have to retrieve my gold crown.

THE BACKSIDE PLAN

I knew what I had to do. I had no choice but to retrieve what I had swallowed, because I could not afford to replace it. The only question was how to logistically pull this off. Obviously, all I needed to do was just poop in a bag. But what kind of bag? And what would I do about peeing? I didn't want to pee and poop in the same bag, It would make my excrement excessively liquidy, messy, and increase the odds of a disaster. Then I got to thinking about what I would do when I was at work? What if I had to go when I was at school? The idea of pooping in a bag did not seem like a particularly positive activity I would want to do outside of the privacy of my own home. Imagine what someone might say if they were to walk into the Chuck-E-Cheese's men's room and find the assistant manager coming out with a Ziploc bag full of poop, finger indents all over it from pushing and squishing the poop around as though he was playing with brown organic Play-doh. Not a particularly pretty sight to envision. The next question was how big of a bag I would need? I'm pretty average to below average in height and weight. And yet, I have never really stared at the bottom of the toilet bowl after taking care of my business and thinking to myself what size Ziploc bag would adequately store my bowel movement. Having put some thought into it, my first assumption was I wouldn't really need that big of a bag. I am not a gigantic dumper, I believe I am a relatively normal size guy with a relatively normal diet. I decided a quart size bag was more than sufficient. However, during my first dry run (a figure of speech in this case), I came to realize that the smaller the bag was in size, the more my hands were having to be held closer to my rectal area. This created a bit of discomfort and awkwardness. It is not every day that you experience the weight of your bum and body pressing down on your wrists and forearms all the while trying to hold open a Ziploc bag and concentrate so you can poop. This walk-through (again, figure of speech) also brought to my attention that I don't have particularly long arms. When you have to sit in the seated position but also curl your arms underneath your butt hole to hold a bag in a consistent place so that your softserve organic chocolate ice cream dispenser will go into the goody bag, you come to the realization of how long or stubby your arms truly are. And I was so afraid about not getting 100% of the poop in the bag. I feared that the inactivity of my arms and the weight that was pressing against them would result in a lack of blood and oxygen flow and inevitably put my arms to sleep. That would lead to me dropping the poop bag into the toilet bowl full of urine and then I would have to dig it out and mash it up while looking for one small gold crown in the midst of the mess. So it was quickly decided that a gallon or extra large gallon Ziploc heavy duty triple zip bag would be needed to carry out this activity with some level of comfort, convenience, and peace of mind.

The next challenge I had to overcome was how to hold a bag in place beneath my butt hole but also avoid spraying it with warm urine. I had to be mindful of not having the bag drag so low that it was submerged in the toilet water. Finally with all of this going on, I still had to concentrate, relax, control the flow and pressure of my pee. And even when I had resolved these challenges and hurdles, the inevitable question still remained of what I would actually do when I retrieved my gold crown. That and, how long would it take before it went through my system?

The Retrieval

So the great Gold Rush of 1998 started. And I waited, and waited, and waited. In addition to waiting, I had to be subjected to all types of conversations, jokes, and awkward looks by my roommates ... and of course by my fiancé, What at that exact moment must've been going through her mind, I could not say. How much or how little information she chose to share with others, roommates, coworkers, her parents back home... I couldn't say. My latest project wasn't something that we necessarily made the center of our conversation.

I don't recall the first time I had to go to the bathroom. All I remember was grabbing a Ziploc bag which I am pretty certain I had stationed close to the bathroom. It was crunch time; it was gametime. So there I sat partially hovering over the toilet seat holding an extra large gallon Ziploc bag. I don't recall how long or how much, but I do remember the first challenge or unprepared scenario that came up, was that once I was finished, I didn't know how I was going to wipe my bottom and then scan whatever poop was on the toilet paper to make sure my gold crown wasn't dangling on it. I had to set the bag down, use toilet paper, and then look over it. After that, I picked up the still opened Ziploc bag and sealed it shut, while trying to get as much of the air out as possible so that as I squished it back and forth so as to avoid a large air bubble that may accidentally pop from too much pressure. I hadn't realized until I was doing it how warm poop is when you touch it. That was the first thing that really struck me. The second thing that resonated with me was that I would have to be extremely precise to ensure each bowel movement had been thoroughly checked to guarantee there was no gold crown hiding. Did I just press with my palm or grip with my hands. No, it was thumb to index finger, pinching every centimeter of poop, visually and physically making sure that a gold crown was not in that bag and it wasn't getting squished or pushed aside. Every inch of dumpage needed to be thoroughly inspected. Consequently, this actually took a lot longer then I anticipated. And as I am going through all of this, I can only imagine what my soon-to-be-bride Julie was thinking. I wondered if this was three months into our relationship, would she be having some serious second thoughts. Seeing how it was three months before our marriage, I wonder if she had reached or past the point of no return. Would she bail now that she knew her soon-to-be husband was willing to poop in a Ziploc bag to find something that he would inevitably put back in his own mouth. In retrospect, it would be hard for me to fault anybody, and not just Julie, for having second thoughts about marrying such a person.

Unfortunately, the first bowel movement came up empty. Obviously it didn't come up empty. There was plenty to sort through, but I don't recall finding anything substantial or noteworthy. So while I am sure there was a level of disappointment, I also was prepping myself for the possibility that it could be several bowel movements before my gold crown was found. The thought did cross my mind, however, about what I would do if I never found my crown. What if it never exited? How long was I going to poop in a bag? Was I going to do this for a week, three days, a month? I really did not have an answer, But those questions did surface.

After being unsuccessful on my first try, I took the Ziploc bag of poop outside and threw it in the apartment dumpster. I was not about to have one bag of poop just sitting idly in a garbage can inside the apartment. This routine went on for a couple days to the point where my entire routine became habitual. It quickly became a side note, instinctual, and it was a little unsettling how easily I became accustomed to holding a bag, pooping in a bag, having the ability to urinate in the toilet while missing the bag to make sure there wasn't any splatter.

And then, on the third day, as if it was some kind of biblical rising from the dead, I felt something hard as I pinched and squeezed the Ziploc bag. There was something that did not belong in a bag of poop... It was my gold crown! All of my labor, all of my time and mental energy that I had put into devising this plan and executing it, I had found my golden ticket. Victory was mine... but that euphoria quickly went away when I realized that I now had to retrieve it out of the bag. I would have to reach in and grab it out of the bag full of poop. The whole purpose of this exercise was not just to find my gold crown but to reunite it with my back right molar. And even before I took the plunge to retrieve it from the bag, I started to question what I would need to do in order to clean it, sanitize it, and mentally overcome the knowledge that I was putting the gold crown that had passed through my entire body back into my mouth. I had to decide what I needed to do in order to make it okay in my brain to shove it back in my mouth. I went to the local grocery store and purchased some household cleaner, pure rubbing alcohol, and maybe even bleach... I can't completely recall with 100% accuracy. After rinsing all of the poop out of the crown, I plopped it into a paper cup and poured some type of chemical cocktail and let it soak for a few days. And then, when I was satisfied... I put it back on my right molar, kissed my fiancé, and three months later... I got married.

And a little while later, I believe I swallowed a gold crown again. And that time, I just let it go. My wife made a vow "for better or for worse" but I've been told there's only so much crap a wife can take ... literally.

A LITTLE ABOUT JONATHAN:

Jonathan is the modern day Moses for Korea. Smuggled out of Seoul at an early age, he was adopted by an American family, not knowing he was Asian royalty. Unlike the Biblical Moses, Jonathan has yet to return to his homeland to deliver his people or grow a beard - but he hopes someday to do both. In his Gentile life, Jonathan Hetterly, MA, LPC, works with teenage and young adult males, specializing in treating substance abuse, addiction, and failure to launch struggles. He contributed to The Walking Dead Psychology and Star Wars Psychology. Follow him at @jhetterly or Shrink-Tank.com, and hear him on the "Shrink Tank" and "Change Your Tune" podcasts.

Tell Me Why You Came In Here Today

Kristin Daley

"Tell me why you came in here today. What is going on with Kristin?" The psychologist appeared cool and almost smug. Her office was in an elegant building in Dilworth, a rich suburb of Charlotte; one of the prettiest buildings I had ever seen. She sat in her large chair, while me and my parents were spread between a sofa and a chair, me in the chair. My mom had driven me to the appointment, and explained that this was the same psychologist who was treating a few of my friends, so likely someone who understood troubled teens like me. It was a nauseating conversation, as I sat quietly in the passenger seat.

Mom and I had not been on good terms for much of my life, and it was unlikely to start to get better anytime soon. One of the major life lessons my mother imparted on me was to trust no one. My mother frequently made me the butt of her jokes; she indicated in various ways that I was too unattractive or foolish to ever become anything worthy of love.

Lesson 1: (age 6) "Let's make Barbie a wedding dress because we know that she is pretty enough to get married one day."
Lesson 2: (Repeated often between ages 4-12) "You are a bull in a china shop!"
Lesson 3: (age 11, in a dressing room trying on a new outfit) Mom, laughing, "You look like the side of a house!"
Lesson 4: (repeated throughout my life, but most often when I was disappointed by a rejection of some sort) "Kristin, in life there are race horses and there are work horses. You will always be a work horse." This statement was usually followed by a quick segue to a discussion about her grandfather's work on a farm with draft horses, further tying together the concept that my body more closely resembled that of a draft horse.

I always felt justified in my lack of trust toward her.

"Well," my Dad took a deep breath, "she has been having sex, doing drugs, and lying to us." The therapist coolly nodded and jotted notes, while my mother's jaw fell open and she locked a stony stare on me. Dad had kept my personal information to himself, as promised, until this moment. Now it was out in the open.

The conversation had started between Dad and I several weeks earlier. He had taken me on a "surprise" hiking trip to the top of Mount Mitchell. We had started a hike, and then stopped near the peak to sit on a bench. Dad told me that he felt that this trip was the best way to talk to me about his concerns about my behavior. He had read my journal, the gig was up, and he wanted me to explain myself. The funny/sad fact was that I had started the journal because I felt misunderstood by my mother, and wanted to keep a record of my own experiences so that my own daughter would some day know that I understood how hard it was to be a teenage girl. I had not intended any other audience than this imaginary future daughter, and now Dad had read it. He told me that he was aware that I was sexually active and doing drugs, and wanted to know how he could help me change. I had told him that it was my life, and there was no need for me to change; I was a straight A student with afterschool activities who managed to stay very intoxicated/high every weekend. I wanted to be free to make my own mistakes.

"How long has this been going on?" All three heads shifted their gaze to me. Mom's face was stuck in her angry glare, a look with which I had long been familiar, Dad's expression was a combination of hopeful and encouragement, while the therapist sustained her look of detached interest, almost boredom- this was not a new dynamic to her.

"We don't really know. She has been lying to us for a very long time." My Dad gave his best effort to break the silence. Again the look of pleading encouragement.

To me, the issue of not being a normal kid in our family started around the age of five. When I was five, my brother pointed at my belly in my bikini and informed me that I was fat. It was a devastating word. This was followed at the age of eight, when my parents also informed me that my weight was becoming a problem. Their attempt at a solution was weighing and body measurements in the family living room, followed by recommendations that I avoid the soda, chips, and cookies that my mom was buying for my brothers. "Those are not for you. Foods can make you fat. Remember, Kristin, fluffy buns will give you fluffy buns." Dad was diabetic, and stated that his main concern was that I would be diabetic too if they didn't intervene soon. Mom appeared to be disturbed by how unattractive being overweight made me. In looking at pictures of me, I was on the upper end of normal, but I was not where I needed extreme intervention, especially by today's standards.

"What was Kristin like as a young child? Any challenges with her when she was younger?" Mom explained that I managed to hit all of my developmental milestones on time, even if I was slow to fully embrace potty training, a fact that she always seems to enjoy. Dad explained that I was always academically gifted and pretty talkative.

My family identified me from an early age as being a fantastic liar. I use the term "fantastic" because there was some craft and flair to the lies that were told, but I think that they probably would have simply preferred "liar" or maybe "compulsive liar" if you insisted on a descriptive term. I can say that my lying usually related to two different circumstances: 1) I did not feel that I had the interpersonal skills to explain my point so a lie would work in place of these skills, or 2) I just lied because that was the first thing that came out of my mouth.

Around the age of five, my father traded his job as a high school math teacher and basketball coach for a more exciting and high-salary job as a computer programmer. This started a long career for him with many tech jobs and many moves for our family. The first move was to Tulsa, and my father moved almost a year in advance so that he could complete his training in computers. I liked Tulsa, because it was wild and we were given a lot of freedom. I walked to school across a pretty big field, and was able to collect lots of stray animals during my daily commutes. I kept a piece of rope in my backpack, would drag whatever animal I had found to my home, remove the rope, and explain that the dog/cat/rabbit had followed me home. My parents were animal-lovers; we had quite the menagerie by the time I finished my first grade year. Some of the dogs were aggressive, so we were unable to play in our backyard, but I enjoyed having them there. There was a real problem with fire ants in Tulsa, and my buddy and I decided that we would save the neighborhood from the ants. We took some of his father's tools from his garage, went to the largest ant pile we could find, and started hacking away at it with the tools. In a matter of seconds, we were both covered in fire ants and screaming as we ran home. "Attack out of the blue" was my explanation for this event, which resulted in my buddy being hospitalized.

How does she get along with her siblings? I watched for how they would respond to this one, because it was a sore spot for me. My brother was always my mother's favorite, while I remained my Dad's favorite. My younger brother, sadly, was often left to his own devices. Mom and Dad both tried to explain that the relationship could be tough at times. Dad expressed that it has always been important to him to see us get along. I responded with, "Usual stuff."

Around the age of eight, I developed my "anger problem," but I feel that it was likely brewing for a long time before then. My older brother had a tendency to find my head to be in the right/wrong place when he was using shovels or baseball bats, and had inflicted a good bit of damage on me through the years. I had achieved some good revenge when I tripped him in our Tulsa house, and he landed headfirst into our marble windowsill- "accident" was my simple explanation and "concussion" was the outcome. In Michigan we discovered cross-country skiing and my parents gave us all of the necessary equipment. We used the ski poles more for beating each other and long-distance poking than we ever did for actual skiing, but it was still some degree of sport. My brother also liked to play "professional wrestler" and used this as a good excuse to give me a pounding. When my ears were newly pierced, he was repeatedly slamming my head into the carpet and one of the earrings got caught on a loop in the carpet. It was ripped out of my ear, and my father came in to see what the raucous was. His version of punishment was trying to jump on my brother, who kept rolling just out of his reach. Eventually, they fell into giggles, and my ear was forgotten. My "anger problem" reached its apex when I slammed my younger brother's head in the car door. My mom, who had a degree in early child development and fancied herself a child psychologist, insisted that I start keeping a journal of what makes me mad. "You can draw pictures if you don't have the words to express it." I had the words, but the whole thing felt futile- what did it matter if I wrote about how much my brother hurt me, when they seemed to find it to be amusing more than distressing? At that time, younger brother was the safe target.

When I was about to enter the third grade we were moving to another state, and I had become old enough to stop viewing these moves as an adventure and see them more as a source of distress. Virginia was mostly a pretty great place to live, and we were in one of those self-contained communities that had a pool and elaborate playground. My parents let me walk to school by myself and the usual hijinks ensued. I often walked home via the large creek that ran through the neighborhood, and would skip from stone to stone in the water. I called it "creek-walking" and it was the reason most of my shoes were quickly ruined. My mother would demand that I not go in the creek, but I usually had some reason why this had to happen- saving a dog from the river or collecting trash to maintain the neighborhood, whatever prosocial idea came to mind. My brother started middle school, which created some break in the constant fighting between us- he now had my Dad to fight with as he decided he would rather ride his skateboard than play basketball. The day he came home with a Mohawk was seriously one of the best days of my life, because it seemed that everyone was finally mad at him. The fact that it looked ridiculous was merely a bonus.

Our time in suburban paradise came to an end after about 3 years, when a family trip to Florida was actually a house-hunting excursion for our next move. In preparation for our relocation, my mother took me to the barber who cut my brother's hair. Both of my brothers had flat-top, military-style haircuts (reaction to the Mohawk incident), and this barber was very affordable. Mom explained that he spoke no English, but you just showed him a picture of the desired haircut, and he would perform it. I brought in the picture of my cute haircut- the promo shot of Molly Ringwald for "Pretty in Pink." The barber grunted at the picture, and started the haircut. It turns out that he actually only performed flat-top haircuts, and we came to that sick realization after the haircut was pretty much finished. I was devastated. I had been in the ugly pubescent stage that I swear all girls go through, and now I had the flat-top to go with it.

"How does Kristin do with her peers? Has she been able to develop friendships at school?" All eyes again fixed on me, and I again responded with a short answer.

First day at my new school in Florida was painful, to say the least. My parents had enrolled me in a Catholic school, and I was the strange, large girl with a boy's haircut. People weren't lining up to be my friend and even the girl who was given the task of showing me around seemed pretty angry about it. I went weeks with nary a conversation and prayed that my hair would grow and somehow divine intervention would allow me to fit in. The few misfits in my grade slowly allowed me into their fold, which was likely related to pity and their overall lack of friends. We moved there in November, and no one, not a single person from my class, attended my birthday pool party in April. I spent the occasion locked in my room, listening to "Under Pressure" by Queen on repeat.

After a couple of years in middle school hell, I started high school with a whole new cohort of people. My older brother had been the cool guy in high school and I started the year with some positive social credibility thanks to being his kid sister. I also had gone through a growth spurt over the summer, and my hair was finally significantly more feminine. I started the year with a clean slate, and was able to quickly shed some of the negative images that my classmates might have carried from my 6th grade year. I had friends, I laughed, and I danced at dances- I was even invited to Cotillion! It was glorious. About mid-way through this amazing year, the news came. Dad had been transferred to Charlotte, and we would be moving over the summer. He was relocating immediately, and my mom was left with the task of selling our house and maintaining three children who were devastated. My older brother would be enrolling in community college, so he was spared the relocation. I was so jealous of his dingy first apartment and ability to maintain friends. To say that I went wild for the remainder of the year would be an understatement. I discovered that alcohol numbed me out, and guys were starting to be really drawn to my less awkward body.

Under extreme duress, I was moved over the summer before my sophomore year of high school. Mom and Dad reminded me that high school started in 10th grade at my new school, so this would not be as bad of a transition as the previous moves. My younger brother was struggling just as much as I was (and just as awkward as I had been when we moved to Florida, shitty haircut included). I decided he would be my favorite person, and I would be kind to him. He was so desperate for love and affection that he quickly became my shadow, and I mothered him every chance I got. When we drove to our new house in Charlotte, I was excited to see that it was at least very close to a mall. "No, Kristin, that is not a mall, that is a church," was my father's response. "Welcome to the south." I came up with a strategy for adjusting to this new school- I would smile at everyone and make friends through my utter kindness. This strategy lasted about two hours into my first day of school when a girl who clearly was very popular glared at me and asked what I was smiling about. Second strategy, I joined the varsity swim team to try to stay in shape and as an effort to make more friends. Most of the swimmers on the team were part of an external competitive league, and skipped our practices, so it was pretty ineffective. Third strategy, making friends with guys first, was much more effective.

"Drug use? Sexual activity?" The therapist was still trying to draw information. My curt responses did not seem to answer her questions about my history, and my father seemed anxious to have me be the one to tell the story. I think he realized that he had messed up pretty big time with my mom by promising to keep my secrets private from her. I am really not sure what he was thinking or what I was thinking when I agreed to talk. I think that being on the side of a mountain, with no escape, had affected my thinking.

After we moved to Charlotte, my lies became more intense and about more significant issues. A common activity in Charlotte in the early 1990's was throwing parties in hotel rooms. It was very decadent to be able to drink and party the night away without a single parent to come and wreck the situation. At one party, I met the guy who would be the eye of my downward spiral hurricane and my mentor into the world of drug use. I had been out dancing with a guy and we had landed at this hotel party. We were drunk, as was everyone else in the room. This guy threw an ashtray at me, and stated that my smiling made him uncomfortable. I was smitten. We went to the same high school and I would see him in the halls. He asked me out at the end of the year. Over that summer, I started smoking, learned to stop eating, and became what I had always dreamed of: skinny and popular. One by one, he introduced me to different drugs, and I enjoyed the uncanny release of substance use.

I also got my license that spring and was even given a car for my sixteenth birthday. To say that I was a good driver would be a significant lie. I have always struggled with judging distances, and this was proven when I was driving my Dad's car one night. I misjudged the distance to get around a city bus, and rear-ended it with the front corner of my car. The busing supervisor had to come out and a thorough police report was documented. The front headlight was the only damage on my car, and there was no damage on the bus, so I decided to explain it to my parents in a simpler fashion, "I came out of the movie and the damage was done to the car, must have happened in the parking lot." My parents were fine about it, until my Dad got the call from the insurance company while he was at work. It turns out that two people on the bus decided to sue us for thousands of dollars in bodily harm and the insurance company needed statements to battle the case. "What tangled webs you weave, when you practice to deceive," my mother used this as a constant admonishment.

My essential and most frequent lie was that I was spending the night at a friend's house. My parents would never verify where I was staying, because they tended to avoid social contacts. I also kept the names on pretty steady rotation, understanding that my parents may want to get to know a friend or their family if they saw them as a frequent fixture in my social sphere. I had sleepovers almost every Friday and Saturday night, and these sleepovers gave me the great freedom to not be at home and have as much fun as I wanted. My experience with driving and the horrific hijinks of absolute freedom in an automobile came to a close after a very short period of time. About 6 weeks after my parents gave me my car, I totaled it in a car accident. My boyfriend ended up soaring into and partially through my windshield; he had always felt too cool for seatbelts. Surprisingly, the insurance company was no longer willing to insure me as a driver, so I had to legally surrender my license; I had been a legal driver for about 3 months.

My parents kept encouraging me to have some people to our house and then came the fated night when I invited a friend over whose mother was assertive enough to reach out and speak with my parents and thank them for the invitation. As the conversation unfolded, my mother thanked her for hosting me on so many occasions. Her mother was dumbfounded, as she was quite certain I had never set foot in their house. My mother's anger grew as she started to calculate the number of times that my whereabouts had been unaccounted. My friend's helpful mother suggested the psychologist who was seeing her daughter, with whom we were now meeting.

"What kind of goals would you have for treatment?" My parents tried to explain that they needed my behavior to come into better form. They found my rebellion to be more in absentia- they knew my behavior was out of control, but much of my life was too secretive to be well addressed. From my perspective, I found it irritating and amusing to watch my parents try to pretend that they had always done a great job being present as parents. Mom explained that she had been a teacher in order to be able to be home with us on summers and prioritized school achievement. Dad did not share that he traveled about 75% of the time for work and usually spent the weekends he was home watching college basketball. They could not say that my grades were an issue, as I was a straight-A student.

The ride home from the first session could have been better. Dad needed to go back to work, which meant that I got to ride alone with mom. After I closed the door, she turned to me with a look that would have easily rivaled Medusa's deadly stare. "How could you share all of that information with your father and not say a word to me? How dare you act like we aren't interested in your life?" The rest of the ride, she accused me of sleeping with every guy who had ever crossed our threshold and any other names she could try to dig up. It was lucky that I had been creative with the names of my friends, because she had a long list with which to work. She mostly harped on the guys she had actually met, and I consistently denied all of them She did not have my trust, and really never would. This would not be the last time my mother accused me of being a slut. My wedding day was the last time, but it was because she felt my choice of wedding dress was slutty, and not that I, at that time, was a slut.

Treatment was established, with the simple goals of me not lying anymore. My father's insurance would pay for four sessions, and then we could re-evaluate. I knew that this psychologist saw several of my good friends, so always wondered what parts of stories she could piece together. Honestly, I had been trained well by my parents to not show fear, weakness or emotions of any sort. My experiences from early childhood had informed me that trusting conditions to change in my house was an exercise in disappointment. Anger was pretty safe, but there was no way I was going to share my anger with this psychologist; it went too deep. I mostly spoke about challenges in my friendships and kept my mouth shut about the bigger issues. After the four sessions, my psychologist determined that she did not feel I was willing to use therapy in an effective manner. You have to open up, trust and share to be a good therapy client, and I was unwilling to do any of that.

I would like to say that I turned around shortly after this episode, but it really took many years, and almost being kicked out of UNC-Chapel Hill for me to really straighten out. When I was completing my pre-doctoral internship, a wise mentor in my program stated that she always encourages undergrads that want to study psychology to go through therapy first. She stated that she thinks that most people who become psychologists do so because they have a lot of their own shit to figure out. I had PhD-level shit.

A LITTLE ABOUT KRISTIN:

Kristin Lamb Daley was born in Hanover, PA, the middle child in her family. They moved several times through her upbringing, and eventually landed in Charlotte, NC, where she has stuck. She briefly escaped Charlotte to attend UNC-Chapel Hill, and remains a Carolina girl through and through. She had long dreamed of being a doctor, so much so that her family used to refer to her as "Dr. Lamb." She started a career in sleep and psychology, and eventually received her doctorate in health psychology from UNC-Charlotte. She still daydreams of attending medical school, possibly after her own children get through school, and insists that people call her Dr. Daley whenever possible.

Bully

Frank Gaskill

I often offer a first, free appointment which allows a prospective client to kick the tires and see if I could be a good fit for them and their family. The question I often hear is when they look around my office and see all the Star Wars and Lego memorabilia is, "Why are you a psychologist?" My answer used to be an easy one which quickly lowered defenses through humor and lack of depth. The patented answer I offered was, "Well, I didn't really know what I wanted to do in college, so a friend of mine suggested I go into the helping field because I had good grades in my psychology courses." The response to my friend was, "That sounds pretty good. I guess I'll try that."

My answer was believable and wrong, but the answer worked and got a laugh. The true answer to the question of why I wanted to be a psychologist was actually unknown and unknowable to me at the time. I was too emotionally immature. But my answer at the time seemed to make sense in my own personal narrative.

Why I became a psychologist was something I didn't fully understand until I was in my late 30's. Many people say psychologists enter their profession to work out their own personal issues. I think they are actually right most of the time about this. But others find a balanced mix. My realization of my purpose in becoming a psychologist underscores the fact that we, most of the time, have no real understanding of why we do what we do. Our motivations are most often unknown and unseen. But while late to the game, I think I really do finally understand my personal, "Why?" My hope is that many others would as well. We do what we do for a reason and not at random. The sins of our fathers are passed to our sons.

I am the only child of an only child. By the time the fourth grade rolled around, I had inhabited my second country and third state and also attended my 7th school. By the way, that second country I lived in should really count as four countries given it was pre-revolutionary Iran. With all of my family's travels, my own personal social survival was at stake. Friendship making skills and blending in were paramount abilities that I had to sharpen. One might think my social skills would have been honed to a razor's edge by age 10. And you would be severely wrong.

Years before, a 4-year old version of myself was standing in the front yard of my parents' home in Kinston, North

Carolina. The road we lived on was typically busy as it led straight to a large mall which was really the only mall for probably 60 miles. So we're talking a lot of traffic was on that road in front of my house. In retrospect, I'm pretty sure that little boy (me) had a vague sense he shouldn't have been anywhere near that busy road. In fact, he likely had been told by his mom repeatedly to not go in the front yard by himself ever. Like Ever! But there I was, standing within 3 feet of busy traffic and staring at every passing car. I was breaking a rule. And I felt powerful.

Few real memories exist from that time other than my love of G.I. Joe and Evel Knievel, a stunt motorcycle guy from the 70's. Evel Knievel was pretty crazy and did some ridiculous stunts breaking most of his bones at one point or another. My obsession with him was to collect all of his action figures and toys, even building a ramp for the toy version of Knievel to jump a ditch in an attempt to recreate his Grand Canyon jump. So you would think if I saw a guy on a Harley motorcycle, I would wave and smile and feel as if I was near a hero. Again, you would be wrong.

Still standing very near the road, a loud Harley with impossibly tall handlebars and a gleaming black gas tank was barreling straight for me. A man in black was at the controls, and he had a pretty girl on the back of his bike which made him seem even more important and powerful. I can still clearly see his painted helmet with the colors of the American flag glinting with metallic flecks against the North Carolina sun. This man and his bike in the early 1970s was the definition of rebel cool. As he passed by, he clearly glanced down at my small face through his dark, round sunglasses. I raised my hand to gesture to him. But instead of waving hello or giving a "thumbs up," I gave this bearded, Harley riding stud with girl in tow the middle finger.

To this day I can still hear the screech of his thick rear tire locking up as he slammed on brakes. I was terrified and frozen with fear as I saw him turn that black bike around. My feet were rooted to the ground. The unbelievably loud Harley pulled up in front of my once safe and innocent home. Inside were all of my trains, cars, and stuffed animals. A big scary world just drove up thanks to my unconscious invitation to tell this guy to, "Go To Hell." I had no idea what I had done other than it was wrong.

The man in black and sunglasses asked, "What was that kid!!!?" I smiled back and raised up my thumb saying, "You're a cool dude." He looked dumbfounded and was literally speechless. Under a summer Carolina sun, what seemed like a half hour passed like an eternity. I continued staring at him and said, "I think your helmet is cool!" The blonde girl on the bike smiled at me. He laughed. Sort of. Firing up his horse, the biker and his blonde took off down the road. The danger had passed.

Running into the backyard of my house, I began crying uncontrollably. Why did I give a stranger the finger? I still don't know. I don't think I even knew what it meant. Maybe it was a TV show or probably a cousin who showed me. But it was my first memory, for good or evil, in which I realized words and gestures mattered and could invite power or terror into my life.

So maybe a little background might help. My parents were pretty busy people, and I had a big imagination. I spent a lot of time with my Legos and Matchbox cars and later could be found burying myself in books most of which were unfortunately Judy Blume books. I was pretty sure I would get a period one day. Some, well maybe everyone, would argue I was a pretty inward looking and an egocentric kid, but occasionally I would get glimpses of myself which were not altogether pretty. Most of the time I was oblivious to these external impressions but am now quite certain everyone else saw my hot mess.

The best feedback I ever received was usually from a teacher, a stranger, or a friend's parent. Social lessons were hard but powerfully learned. My dad said you should always dress up on an airplane. I still do. Sport coats are important, but I have no idea why. Tipping well at a restaurant and standing very patiently in long lines are also behaviorally ingrained into my personality. But interpersonal and subtle social skills were hard for me growing up. I think mainly because I was pretty selfish and self-centered in part due to being an only child and feeling I could be an equal to all the adults with whom I mainly socialized (my parents' friends). My dad usually gave me a good deal of freedom, but not a lot of life instruction came with this freedom. I often ended up in situations which were not conducive to social success. Take Missy for example.

Missy was, in my retrospective mind's eye, a cute girl upon whom I had the biggest crush. She had long hair and a loud laugh. She was somewhat of a Tomboy, kind of like Peppermint Patty from Charlie Brown. We would often ride bikes together and get into pomegranate wars. Growing up in Iran, we found all kinds of ways to entertain ourselves and grabbing handfuls of pomegranates and throwing them at one another was big fun. The red stains the fruit left is proof that I actually invented a primitive form of paintball.

After tagging along with a gang of kids one day, I ended up standing around with them and our bikes just talking about nothing really. There may have been 7 or 8 of us including the beautiful Missy. I recall some of the kids prodding her to ask me something. I was the resident nerd of knowledge, so I figured it had to do with school. "Go ahead and ask him!" a kid blurted out. She was now smiling at me, and I really did not know what to do. I liked her a lot but was too shy to really even admit that feeling to myself much less say anything to her about my crush. Before I knew what was happening, she turned to me and said in a surprisingly confident voice, "Will you go with me?"

I was sort of stunned but also relieved that the question wasn't more complicated than understanding directions to some unknown place. My answer to her question was, "Where are you going?" She returned a blank look. There was a bit of a pause and I heard some giggles. She broke the silence replying, "No, no. Will you GO with me?" I still didn't understand and asked again, "Where?" I perceived a shift in the crowd around me and some not so subtle laughter broke out. I didn't understand what was happening. She asked one more time, "Don't you get it? Will you go with ME!?" And I asked yet again, "But...where...?" I felt a lump in my throat. What was I missing? She looked exasperated, and now the kids were laughing out loud directly at me.

A wave of red heat flushed my body. I had been laughed at a lot, and my escape route was always my bike. I hopped on and took off, tears welling up yet again. I literally had no idea what she or the kids were talking about. Of course I understand now, and I still feel like an idiot. She wanted me to be her boyfriend. Why did I miss that? Her words meant she liked me and there was lot of power and meaning to those words as well as the laughter of those kids. Words conveyed information, and they could hurt too.

Missing out on a date with Missy as a 4th grader wasn't such a big thing. But the slow accumulation of failed social experiences was building and wearing on me. The next few years included a brutal incident of home sickness and being chased by a principal and school nurse across a school parking lot. Those years also brought desperate pleas for attention that included bragging that my dad was the first man on Mars as well as a multitude of stories about my growing up in Iran and other exaggerated tales (I did live in Iran though).

Those stories were sure fire attention getters. However, with such a limited arsenal of stories, my tales grew old. I wasn't aware of my increasingly annoying presence as I was too desperate for friendship and attention. Unconsciously, I decided bad attention was better than no attention. The years dragged on with having my clothes stolen in P.E., my head shoved into toilets, and an unwilling surprise barrel roll in a large trash can. Those were some good times. To say I had no friends didn't quite capture my life during middle school. I was kind of a black hole of friendship, and my event horizon sucked in any abuse possible. I was nobody. But one day, there was hope that maybe I could be somebody.

Ms. Dale approached me after class and stated she would like me to work the lights at the next talent show to be held in the school gym. I was taken aback but very excited. Such an opportunity to contribute! Yes, that's how bad it was. I was excited about working lights at a crappy talent show. But the feeling that I actually could do something seemingly important felt powerful! I shyly said thank you and then became very nervous. I wanted those lights to go on and off without a hitch. Such responsibility had never come my way. Now I wonder if some of the adults had finally taken notice of my low social standing and decided to throw me a bone. Either way, I was thrilled and did not want to screw it up.

The day of the talent show arrived, and I was dressed to kill in my high water khakis, plaid shirt, cloth belt, and tie. I was ready for the lead in an 80's John Hughes film for sure. Those light switches are still burned in my brain. Stainless metal cover fixed against the interior brick of the gym wall with cream colored porcelain switches. There may have been 8 of them but it looked like the control panel of the space shuttle. My piano playing, hardened fingers were ready to flick them on and off with lightning speed when directed to do so by my chorus teacher.

With my hands at the ready and the show about to go on, I suddenly felt hard pressure from behind me as I was slammed against the wall, my fingers pried back off the light switches. Confused and holding fast, I grabbed at the switches, protecting them with both my hands. I was not going to mess this thing up. And it was then I heard the low growl in my ear whispering, "I'm gonna do the lights, Dumbo." That was my nickname at the time due to my enormous ears. Today it's funny. Back then it cut to the bone.

The voice in my ear was my long standing nemesis. He

had been my friend when I first moved to town, but after recognizing my lower social standing, I became meat for his ever hungry need for power and control. His name was Mike, and I just couldn't take it anymore. Some light switch in my head snapped on. Just as I had quickly told the biker I thought he was cool, I now used my words in another way to not only save my butt but to hurt. I snarled back at Mike that I was going to do the lights, and he couldn't stop me. He quickly tried to prove me wrong by wrenching my arm hard behind my back and shoving me forward. Tears broke out quickly and I lost my breath from the pain. At any point I knew my arm would dislocate. But my words snarled forth, and to this day I don't understand from where those words came.

"Mike, you can beat me up all you want, but your parents are still getting a divorce..."

After the words escaped me, the pressure pushing my arm vanished. And so did Mike. He was now running and crying as he unsuccessfully tried to escape my verbal gunshot.

He stayed underneath those bleachers during the whole talent show. I cried and was shaking while I worked those lights. Yes, I was free, but I hurt him.

I knew about his parents' divorce. I had heard stories from my parents' friends. And unconsciously those words stayed there until they burst forth from all those years of hurt. I have never since experienced such power from words, and I still regret allowing them to escape my lips. And those words set me upon a purposeful path allowing me to knowingly answer the question, "Why am I a psychologist?"

I am a psychologist because words are powerful. Sticks and stones will break my bones, but words will never hurt me is crap. I'm pretty sure Mike would have preferred being thrown into a trash can than the dagger of his parents' divorce that I threw brutally into his face. I blindsided him, and yet I never touched him.

And so now I try to do the opposite. My clients are Aspies, and those who live on the Autism Spectrum. They are often the humiliated, clueless, quirky kids that want and desperately need friends. Their families and schools want to help but just don't get it. I am a psychologist because I want to find these kids before they are hurt and guide them through the shark infested waters of middle school. They make me laugh and allow me to teach them from experience and from my own history.

And in all my sessions I make sure that each and every boy I work with knows how to answer a girl when she asks, "Will you go with me?"

A LITTLE ABOUT FRANK:

Having only recently been able to use public restrooms with the help of his iPhone, Dr. Gaskill a.k.a. "Dr. G" is the resident clinically insane person at Southeast Psych. He more or less impersonates a psychologist and is also a contributor to the ShrinkTank podcast as, "The Psych Weasel." Dr. Gaskill actually specializes in Asperger's, effective parenting, and how technology and kids can interface successfully. He is a founding partner at Southeast Psych, one of the largest psychology practices in the United States. Gaskill is also the co-author of Max Gamer (2011, Hero House Publishing), a graphic novel about Asperger's. Drawing on his years of experience in private practice, Gaskill is also focused on his book, How We Built Our Dream Practice: Innovative Ideas for Building Yours which he co-authored with Dr. David Verhaagen.

My Pause Button

Melissa Miller

Growing up during the 90's in Iowa with very support-
ive parents and a story book community, I had never really
met an obstacle I couldn't overcome or move. It would be
fair to say that I didn't face much disappointment in my
formidable years. I felt surrounded by positive encouragement, and nothing seemed too big an obstacle. It was easy to
jump in head first with any idea, big or small, and if it didn't
work, then my cheerleading entourage usually patted me
on the back and swept away the broken pieces. Even when
it came to getting into trouble, I never really had to face the
music. One night in particular stands out to me when I think
about evading discipline. Our high school had a hill next to
the parking lot. Each year the seniors would arrange huge
wood logs to form the numbers of their graduating year. For
some reason, when I was a junior, I thought it was necessary and hysterical to rally my friends to sneak to the hill in
the middle of the night and rearrange the logs to form our
graduating year, 95. Nothing was funnier than watching the
disgruntled seniors putting back their rightful numbers and
hear them grumbling about how cheated they felt and then
deliberate over who could be the culprits.

A warm spring night in May, 1994, I was with 2 girlfriends at the hill around 3:00AM. We had upped our game

with the logs, having bought spray paint in our class colors (red, blue and white), along with little flags to stick in the ground around the newly formed 95. It was all very color coordinated and bursting with school spirit. Somewhere in the middle of our endeavor, we started to hear a faint noise, steadily growing in volume, sounding a bit like an airplane. The lights to the parking lot shut off, and we stood up and looked at each other, questioning what in the world was happening. Suddenly, huge spot lights illuminated us from above, as two police helicopters materialized from the wooded area next to the hill. Of course, being the mature juniors that we were, we all screamed, dropped our cans of spray paint, and scampered to the car as fast as we could. I was the driver, so I screeched out of the parking spot and floored it. Now, had the police cars we hadn't noticed yet not formed a blockade to the parking lot, I'm still certain we could never have lost our helicopter tail. It was a very terrifying moment to be a 16 year old girl staring down what felt like the entire Cedar Rapids, Iowa police force, both on land and air. We knew we were in big trouble.

As we stood in a line next to the police car in handcuffs, we tried to plead our innocent case. We tried to get them to see that it was just a harmless prank, all done in good fun. They then informed us that there was actually a serial graffiti bandit on the loose in our lovely town, and they thought that we were likely said bandit. It may sound like a misdemeanor to you, but in small town Iowa, it was easy to believe that a guilty sentence to being the town's serial graffiti bandit would likely end with us spending the remainder of high school in juvie. Yes, we were terrified. But then we then pulled our Hail Mary: didn't they know who we were? We were more active and involved than any student had ever been at this school. We had just been elected head of the Student Senate, captains of the cheerleading squad, and on the honor roll. Yes, looking back I am ashamed to say that we started listing our high school resume, certain that this would impress them so much that they would instantly release us, and maybe even help us finish the job. I remember them looking incredibly un-impressed, actually, and feeling outraged that these awesome facts didn't seem to hold much weight with the police force. My friend Anne, who is still my partner in crime to this day, then begged them to call our principal Dr. Plageman to vouch for us.

Which they did. At 3:30 in the morning our principal got a phone call from the police explaining that three blonde cheerleaders were being arrested for vandalizing his school's property. The police officer gave him all of our names and was then was quiet for a bit of time. When he hung up, instead of reading us our Miranda Rights, he took out the key to the handcuffs. They let us go. Without a warning, without fingerprints, and with an apology.

So you see, after a lifetime of experiences like this, you start to feel invincible. It seemed that life came with a reset button that could be pushed at any time. I believed that I should indeed try everything and anything. I believed people were on my side, and as long as I could work hard, or do some smooth talking, the world was my oyster. Hence the need to not really think details through, and go all in if it sounds appealing. My senior quote? Go big or go home.

That is, until four years later. It was my junior year at

Colorado State University. I was pursuing a B.S. in psychology and loving it. I had known since middle school that I was going to be a Psychologist, and so the first two years in this major fell right in line with my expectations. I had joined a sorority when I moved cross country to college and was now living in my sorority house with my 50 closest girlfriends. This living situation came with a ton of interesting life lessons, fit for another chapter, and sadly one of them was having my eyes opened to how many girls struggled with eating disorders. I started to suspect that my career calling may not be the FBI psychological profiler for serial killers I had always envisioned myself to be, and instead, I may be an eating disorder specialist who was put in this house of a million crazy females to understand their plight and make a positive dent in this world. (Side note, if you ever meet me in person you will find it very amusing that I ever envisioned myself to be Clarice Starling from Silence of the Lambs. At the age of 37, my heart still races as I walk to my car after dark. Clearly, I had very little self-awareness at the time.)

Thinking through my new career path, I thought that it would probably serve me well to not only major in psychology, but also to minor in nutrition. So the day after I settled on my new career path, I marched down to the administration building to declare my new minor. Armed with my new list of required courses for this nutrition minor, I was excited to sign up. I looked at the list, and noticed that if I was going to graduate on time with this minor I had to take several prerequisite classes during the upcoming spring semester in order to get into the higher level classes the following fall. One of the classes required for a minor was Principles of

Biochemistry, which had the prerequisite class of Organic Chemistry. I felt exhilarated as I signed up for Organic Chemistry, thinking these classes sounded exciting and important, and I couldn't wait to prove that I was game for anything that led to my new career path. I did happen to read that there were some prerequisites to Organic Chemistry as well. I had taken a class called the Fundamentals of Chemistry, which also had a lab, and had not found it to be too difficult. What I hadn't taken were the other two prerequisite classes listed under Organic Chemistry. I remember thinking to myself, "Well, I am sure I will be fine. I really need to take this class now, and I did really well in my first chemistry class. I am sure the prerequisite recommendation is merely a suggestion and not really a requirement." And when I registered for the class over the phone, they actually accepted my request for a seat in the class. This confirmed it! It was not in fact necessary to take all the other classes suggested, and I would in fact be just fine.

Spring semester began, and I sat front and center in the 400 seat auditorium on the first day of Organic Chemistry. I had brought with me my brand spanking new molecular structure kit, and was ready for the challenge. In came my professor, carrying an air with him that reeked of arrogance and frustration that he had to stop his very important life to deal with lowly college students. He started the class by leaning on the counter, arms steady and wide, unyielding, and stared all 400 of us down. The room became so quiet you could hear your neighbor swallow. The heavy doors to the classroom opened with a screaming creak and in walked a late student. Our professor turned his attention to the poor fellow and burned him with his eyes as the student struggled to find an open seat. The professor took off his wire rimmed glasses and cleaned them as he tracked his offender as he made his way down an aisle. Once a seat was finally found, the professor slowly removed a pocket watch from his breast pocket of his vest, opened it and checked his time against the classroom wall clock, and then snapped it shut. It was full of effect, as we all snapped to attention.

As he turned on his heels to begin writing on the white board, my neighbor turned to me and informed me that he was legendary in the chemistry department. Legendary? I hoped he was legendary for being such a brilliant teacher and making such an intimidating class seem like child's play. Then my teacher said his first words. And I had no clue what he said. It turns out my brilliant teacher had an incredibly beautiful accent; English was his second, or maybe third or fourth language. That, coupled with the rapid pace of his speech, I could only make out every couple of words. My jaw dropped open. My stomach sank. What had I gotten myself into?

I left determined to stay on top of the material. Every night I cracked my Organic Chemistry book and built molecular structures. The first test came, and I was in shock as I saw my acceptable grade on the exam. I couldn't believe it, I had actually done well! I hit the town with my friends that night to celebrate my big victory! I started to feel like I was a scientist in the rough, just late to getting exposure on the material. I can still feel the sense of pride and awe after getting that test back. It was incredible.

And that feeling promptly ended when I walked into my next Organic Chemistry lecture. The gist of what I caught from my professor was that we had wrapped up the basic section of the course and it was time to get serious about learning. I froze. So all that I just learned, that was the easy part? My head spun as he scribbled diagrams and numbers all over the board, wildly gesturing as my fellow students furiously took notes and nodded their heads in understanding all the while. That lecture could have been a class taught in Mandarin Chinese. I understood nothing.

If it is possible, each class managed to get a bit worse. I pretended to take notes, and instead left classes with beautiful designs covering my notebook from doodling. At night I "read" the chapters in my text book, but none of them seemed to cover what he was teaching us in class. I brought my molecule set with me everywhere I went, including to the bars with friends. I had the thought that if the molecules were near me at all times, we would bond with each other, and then I would be able to understand how and why they bonded to other particles. And maybe if my friends and I built funny shapes out of them I might actually start to understand those suckers. It was shocking that these awesome theories bore no fruit. I then changed it up and used those little atoms and bonds as something to take out my anger and frustration. It felt good to see them hit the wall or be dropped from my room balcony. The next exam was coming and I was petrified. Instead of pulling serious study hours the night before, I thought it would be more helpful to get a good night sleep so that maybe I would be on my best game and be able to get some partial credit on the test. And for good luck, I slept with my textbook under my pillow...just in case.

The grade I got was nothing to be proud of, but honestly, it was better than I thought I would be able to procure. It wasn't an F, but it was by far the worst grade I had ever gotten on a test in my life. But now the reality hit me that this class, which I clearly was not going to do well in, was going to drag down my GPA which I had worked so hard to keep top notch. I started to panic. What had I done? Why on earth had I not thought this through more rationally? I decided I had to drop the class. Unfortunately, when I went to drop the class I discovered I had missed the drop deadline.

After a few tears I decided that I would just have to discuss this matter with my professor, and once he understood my situation, I was sure he would happily help me drop his class. So I slinked into his office during office hours and began to explain. I was having trouble keeping up. I hadn't taken all of the prerequisites recommended for this class. Science isn't my strong suit. I didn't even know what organic chemistry really meant. I just needed him to give me the get out of jail free card and we could laugh and pretend this whole debacle never happened.

I believe his exact words were, "If you are too stupid to

sign up for this class without having taken the prerequisite courses, then you deserve what is coming." And just like that, I wasn't in Iowa anymore. My reset button disappeared in a puff of smoke. I fought back the tears until I had gotten a good distance from his office and collapsed into a corner sobbing. I felt so embarrassed, defeated, and alone. No one was going to be able to save me. When I got home I called my mom and sobbed to her at length about how unfair the situation was, how mean he was, and how terrible I felt. And after I hung up with my mom, I cried to anyone who would listen for the next few days. I cornered people with my swollen eyes, red nose, and frightened them by ranting and raving about the injustice occurring in my life. I could clear a room pretty fast just by entering during those few weeks.

Feeling stuck, I just buried my head in the sand. I stopped going to class. I sat staring at my book, but wondering what the point of reading it was since it was all gibberish to me. I had given up. I began rescue fantasies that played constantly in my head. I imagined situations that would make my professor feel sorry enough for me, so that he would finally come to his senses and let me out of his class. I fantasized about being hit by a bus on the way to his class and deliberated over the perfect injury. It needed to be an injury that wouldn't be debilitating long-term or life threatening, but worrisome enough to make him see that Organic Chemistry was no longer in my best interest. Two broken legs would be good, but a head injury would be too risky. I created several deaths of imaginary family members and wondered if he would have enough heart to understand how I would need a long grieving process and couldn't be expected to partake in any matter related to Organic Chemistry. I searched the obituaries to find a recently deceased person with the same last name as me so I could use it as evidence. I either didn't have the courage, or enough craziness, to see any of my fantasies to fruition. I didn't go to the next exam. (Side note, we were allowed to drop one test grade during the semester, so this wasn't the worst decision in the world. Although it was very out of character for me.)

As the days passed, my humiliation turned to fear, then anger. I couldn't believe that this rude, arrogant man was going to be my demise. It became crystal clear to me that no one could save me, and nothing was going to change this situation, so I had better pull up my big girl panties and deal with this head on. I went all in.

I started to attend help clinics taught by graduate teaching assistants. These were group settings, so I still felt pretty behind and confused. When I would ask the questions I came armed with, such as, "Now what does Organic Chemistry even mean?" there was usually a sigh of annoyance from other students attending. But I pushed my embarrassment down and kept my focus to hopefully garner some new understanding of molecules. That is, until one of the graduate teaching assistants kindly suggested that I pay a private tutor as I was not at the same level of the other students attending the group. I thanked him for the suggestion, and found myself a tutor. Toby.

At the bargain rate of $50 an hour, Toby became my new best friend. Sweet Toby was as stereotypical of an organic chemistry tutor as it gets. A total geek. He refused to look me in the eye, never made any conversation outside of the chemistry material, and cracked science jokes that I never realized were jokes until he would break into silent snorting laughter. Still, I was so thankful for Toby and his willingness to teach me, I would always give him a courtesy laugh. I spent the remainder of that semester spending a ton of time with Toby and working extra shifts at work on the weekends to make the money to foot the bill for my new geeky sidekick. I think we both found it to be a mutually beneficial relationship. When money got a little tight on my part, and I suggested that we may need to start meeting less frequently, Toby had a great compromise. We could keep our current schedule, and he would reduce his rate by half, if we could move from our current meeting place in the chemistry building basement to the dining room of my sorority house. Yep, sweet Toby was exactly that stereotypical organic chemistry tutor nerd, and I sold my sorority sisters out to buy myself some more time with him.

We started meeting during study hours at my sorority house, and poor Toby wore his uncomfortableness like a neon flashing beer sign nailed to his chest. His face was bright red from the second he entered the back gate to the minute that he left. He whispered in a frantic screech that I struggled to hear, since he always had his chin glued to his chest. My friends, of course, thought that this was endearing, sweet, and hilarious, and so they couldn't help themselves from taking the opportunity to come over and attempt to engage him in conversation. They would sing hello to him, try to ask him personal questions, and rub his back while thanking him for helping their friend in such a hard class. Toby's reaction always seemed strange to me. He would answer them very matter of fact, but somewhat harshly, coming off very rude and annoyed. But once a girl would walk away from the interaction, he would break into a huge goofy grin, and then struggle to conceal his expression. He loved it. He adored it. To me, it felt very dirty to witness.

My days with Toby were drawing to an end, as my cumulative final exam drew near. I thanked Toby profusely for his patience and help tutoring me, and I asked for him to wish me luck. His response was something like this: "There is no such thing as luck. And how you do on the final is not a reflection of my knowledge of the material, but of your understanding of the material. So, I don't know how you will do." What sweet parting words. Thank you for the vote of confidence, Toby.

And it had all come down to this grade. Walking into the building to sit for my exam, I could hear the Rocky Theme song blasting around me, building up my energy for the fight. I was in the zone. My heart raced as adrenaline surged through my body for the two hours it took me to finish the exam. I had brought 10 sharpened pencils with me, and they looked like my arsenal of weapons to kill the exam. I whispered the questions to myself and whispered my thought process out loud, just to make sure I was really working through things. I got a lot of aggravated looks from my neighbors, but I didn't care. All that mattered was that I pass this class.

I had to wait 6 days for grades to be posted. As this was pre-on-line days, the school had an automated phone system where you could call and use your student I.D. to hear your semester grades listed. Even though I knew they would not be posted until the following Monday at the earliest, I still started calling every hour, on the hour, the day after the exam. It was torture. Waiting was the hardest part. Grades slowly started to trickle in, but every time the computerized voice would only say, "Organic Chemistry: Grade Not Yet Available." Then I would collapse and contemplate paying the professor a visit. Until finally, one night, eight days later, I heard the computerized voice say, "Organic Chemistry: C."

C. C? C! I had the most conflicted response I have ever experienced receiving this grade. I had never gotten a C before. But I had never had to fight for a grade so hard before. And I passed. I decided it was the most well deserved C there ever had been. It was the only C I got in college, yet it is one of the grades I feel the most proud of. The lasting learning was not chemistry material, because I don't remember anything from that miserable class, but instead the life lesson I walked away with. I learned the hard way that there is no reset button in daily life, so I decided to build in a personal pause button. While it is not my natural tendency to take a deep breath and slow down before I act, I am aware that it serves me well. It is a huge relief to not have to dig myself out of holes made from impulsive decisions. It can be a struggle for me to press my pause button, so I work really hard to make sure that it is a screeching florescent beacon so that it catches my attention when I get excited, toes at the end of the high dive, ready to jump in head first with an idea. My pause button screams things like, "Wait! Think this through!" and "Have you really thought through all sides?" and "Slooooooooooow it down missy!" So I would like to take this opportunity to thank my dear Organic Chemistry teacher for showing me what happens when stupid decisions are made. I learned more from you than you will ever know.

A LITTLE ABOUT MELISSA:

Melissa Miller is a licensed Psychologist who specializes in treating eating disorders and women's issues. After attending Colorado State University, she completed her doctorate in clinical psychology at the University of Denver. Today she lives in Charlotte, North Carolina, where she practices at Southeast Psych. She enjoys spending time with her husband and two children, cooking, running, playing pranks on people, and occasionally writing.

ALSO FROM HERO HOUSE
PUBLISHING

HEROHOUSEPUBLISHING.COM